SPRING

Before you begin

- Always take great care with sharp tools such as scissors, needles and knives.
- Always cover work surfaces with newspaper before you start to paint or varnish your work.
- When using a craft knife always cut away from hands. Use thick card or something similar under whatever you are cutting. Cut slowly and lightly several times.
- Wash your hands and wear an apron before preparing food.

Some basic tools and materials:
paint and brushes
varnish
glue
scissors and craft knife
paper
card
coloured pencils
felt-tip pens

This caterpillar will be crawling through the pages with you. See if you can spot it each time.

Keep coloured foil from sweets and Easter eggs – smooth it out and keep it somewhere safe. Use it to decorate the eggs on pages 4 and 5.

Look for flowers to press and use to make the cards on page 3. Choose perfect flowers with nice long stems. Remember only to pick one or two wild flowers where several are growing.

Pressed flowers

Flowers can be preserved for ever by pressing all the moisture out of them. When picking wild flowers remember to leave plenty for other people to enjoy.

What you will need
★ flowers
★ blotting paper, and flower press or heavy books!
★ card or paper
★ glue and brush

1

Make sure your flowers are undamaged. Arrange them on blotting paper. Cover with more paper.

2

Press with flowerpress or use heavy books as weights. After a few days check to see if the flowers are dry.

3

When completely dry remove carefully. Cut paper or card to make pictures or greeting cards. Arrange flowers and glue into place.

TIP
Cover flowers with sticky-backed plastic to protect them.

Don't be afraid to stick some flowers upside down or sideways.

Bookmarks make great gifts.

Cut out patterned paper to make vase or pot shapes.

For a calendar, add a loop of ribbon, border and small calendar. (Get them from newsagents or stationers.)

3

Painted and stained eggs

Blowing eggs

You can make beautiful Easter egg decorations to hang on a small branch. First you need to prepare the eggs.

What you will need
★ eggs
★ needle
★ small bowl

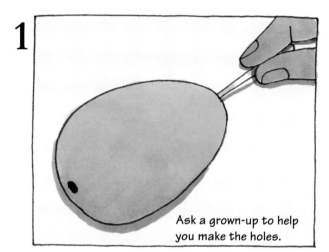

1

Ask a grown-up to help you make the holes.

Make a small hole with a needle at the narrow end of each egg and a larger hole at the other end.

2

Hold the egg carefully over a bowl and blow through the smaller hole. Use the eggs later for baking or scrambled eggs.

For decorating your eggs:
- paints
- felt-tip pens
- brushes
- matchsticks
- thread
- thin ribbons and tassels
- masking tape
- coloured foil
- glue
- small pictures

Tie some thread around a matchstick making a long loop. Gently push the matchstick through the larger hole and hang up.

Fabergé eggs

A Russian jeweller called Carl Fabergé made famous Easter eggs out of precious metals and marble. They were decorated with pearls and diamonds and often contained a secret message!

What you will need
★ blown eggs
★ paints and brushes
★ ribbon or braid
★ glue
★ sequins and jewels
★ section of cardboard tube

Glue loop down.

Paint each egg in a bright colour. Leave to dry.

Glue ribbon or braid around each egg. Glue on a second piece leaving enough to form a loop at the top of the egg.

Glue sequins and jewels all over the egg between the ribbon. Glue one large jewel at the bottom.

Cut out small pictures to glue on to egg.

You can decorate hard-boiled eggs as well but do not eat them once decorated.

Cut small shapes out of masking tape and stick on egg. Paint over egg and remove tape when dry.

Paint and decorate a section of cardboard tube to display eggs.

Glue thin ribbons around egg and a tassel on to the bottom.

Roll coloured foil into balls and squiggles and glue on to painted egg.

Perfect pancakes

Pancakes are delicious with sweet or savoury fillings.

What you will need

To make 6 large pancakes

★ 100 g plain flour
★ large pinch of salt
★ 1 egg
★ 250 ml milk
★ butter for frying
★ fillings (see picture 4)

- sieve
- mixing bowl
- measuring jug
- wooden spoon
- frying-pan

1

Sift the flour and salt into the mixing bowl. Add the egg and half the milk. Mix well to make a smooth batter.

2

Add the rest of the milk and leave the batter to rest for 20 minutes. Meanwhile choose your filling.

3

Put the batter in the jug to make pouring easier.

Cook for 2-3 minutes each side.

With a grown-up helping, heat a knob of butter in the frying-pan. When hot pour in enough batter to cover base of pan. Turn once.

4

chocolate sauce   grated cheese or ham

jam

sugar and lemon

Add cheese or ham to the pancake when it's still in the frying-pan or a sweet filling when the pancake is on your plate.

Egg one out

Each of these eggs has a pair – except one.
Can you spot the odd one out?

Growing seeds

Cress

Growing your own salad cress is easy. It only takes a few days before it is ready to eat.

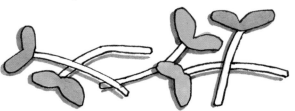

What you will need

★ packet of cress seeds
★ paper towel
★ plate
★ water

1

Place several layers of paper towel on the plate and sprinkle it with water until damp. Scatter seeds on top. Place on a light windowsill.

2

Keep seeds and paper damp and watch the cress grow. When grown, cut with scissors and eat.

Eggheads
Draw faces on broken eggshells and keep upright with a small piece of plasticine. Push some crumpled paper towel down inside the shells. Dampen it, sprinkle on some cress seeds and watch the 'hair' sprout.

Serving suggestions:
Egg and cress sandwiches. Mix it into salads.

Mung beans

Grow your own beansprouts in a jam jar. They take about a week to be ready to eat. Keep them in the fridge once they're ready.

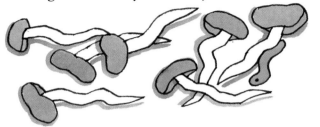

What you will need

- ★ dried mung beans
- ★ sieve
- ★ bowl
- ★ glass jam jar
- ★ water
- ★ piece of net or muslin
- ★ rubber band or string

1

Wash the beans in the sieve under a cold tap. Leave them in a bowl of water overnight. Drain.

2

Put the beans into the jam jar and tie the piece of net or muslin over the top using the rubber band or string. Rinse out beans with water, drain and place on a sunny windowsill.

3

Continue rinsing and draining the beans until all have sprouted. Rinse and eat.

Serving suggestion:
Add to salads – served with a dressing.
Honey and Lemon Dressing
2 tbsp lemon juice
1 tbsp runny honey
$1\frac{1}{2}$ tbsp olive oil
pepper and salt
Put all the ingredients in a screw-top jar. Shake to mix.

Zigzag card

What you will need

★ plain paper and tracing paper
★ pencil, felt-tip pens or paint and brushes
★ scissors

1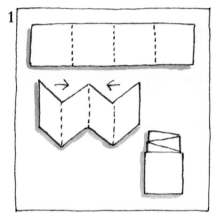

Cut paper into a strip 40 cm long and 9 cm wide. Fold into four.

2

Draw on a cockerel using template and instructions on page 11. Cut out.

3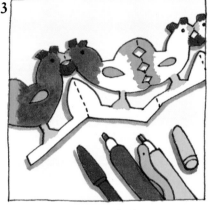

Open out and decorate with felt-tip pens and/or paint.

Eggshell card

What you will need

★ plain card and tracing paper
★ glue
★ eggshells, broken into small pieces
★ pencil, felt-tip pens or paint and brushes

1 Cut card into a piece 22cm x 11cm.

Leave the egg out.

Cut card to size and fold. Draw on a cockerel using template on page 11.

2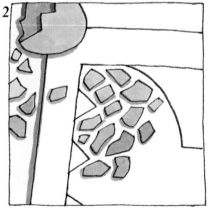

Cover the cockerel shape with glue and then eggshells. Leave to dry.

3

Paint or felt-tip around cockerel and decorate the border.

Wool card

What you will need

★ plain card and tracing paper
★ pencil
★ glue
★ thick coloured wool
★ small black bead

1

2

Push strands close together.

3

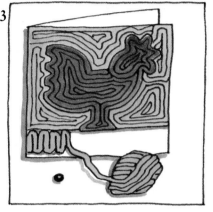

Cut card into a piece 22 cm x 11 cm and fold. Draw on a cockerel using template below. Leave egg out.

Cover the cockerel shape with glue. Starting at the top, carefully cover it with wool.

Glue and cover the rest of card in different colours until finished. Glue bead on for eye.

Trace template on to tracing paper.

Turn over and scribble over the shape with a soft pencil.

Turn over and tape into position on paper or card. Draw over lines.

Easter customs and traditions

Easter is the most important Christian festival. On Easter Sunday Christians celebrate the Resurrection – this was Jesus' return to life three days after he died on the cross.

Passover is a spring festival celebrated by Jews remembering how God rescued the Jews from slavery under the Egyptians.

Long before Christian times people held festivals to mark the end of winter and the beginning of spring. The word Easter probably comes from *Eastre* – the goddess of spring.

Easter eggs are given and eaten in many countries – they are a symbol of new life. Children in some countries believe that the Easter rabbits bring the eggs. Decorating eggs is a custom followed all over the world.

Egg-rolling is a popular game in England and America. An annual contest takes place on the lawns of the White House in Washington, DC. Try egg-rolling with your friends using hard-boiled, decorated eggs. The first egg to reach the finish is the winner.

Easter has no fixed date. Easter Sunday falls between March 22nd and April 25th. It is the first Sunday after the full moon on or after March 21st.

Egg hunts are fun too. Hide small sweet and chocolate eggs either inside or outside in a garden or park. Collect them in small pots or baskets (see the centre section of the book).

Easter is a time for feasting and enjoying traditional foods. **Hot Cross Buns** were originally eaten on Good Friday (the day Jesus died) and they have a cross on top.

Simnel cake is a fruit cake with marzipan on top decorated with marzipan balls representing the twelve Apostles.

Lamb symbolizes Jesus (the 'Lamb of God') and lamb-shaped cakes are popular in some European countries.

Easter parades provide an opportunity to show off new clothes and fancy Easter bonnets. Thousands join in the parade along 5th Avenue in New York City.

Make an Easter bonnet yourself by decorating a hat with paper streamers, ribbons, flowers, chicks and rabbits' ears.

Paper flowers

What you will need

★ crêpe or tissue paper
★ scissors
★ thin wire
★ green paper
★ glue
★ twigs

1

fringed edge

scalloped edge

Cut crêpe or tissue paper into 13 cm x 4 cm strips. Cut some long edges into scallops, some into fringes.

2

Open petals out. →

Holding the straight edges of strips roll up and tightly wind 5 cm length of wire around the bottom edge, leaving some free.

3

Cut leaf shapes from green paper and glue to twigs. Wind the wire round the twigs to attach flowers.

Hanging eggshells

See if you can collect some eggshells.
When painted they make lovely
decorations and look very festive
when hung from a vase full of
dry branches.

What you will need

★ eggshells
★ paint, varnish (if you want) and brushes
★ needle and wool
★ small branches

1

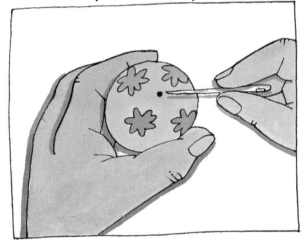

Carefully break round the
edges to make a half shell.

Paint your half shells with a variety
of bright colours and patterns.
Leave to dry. Varnish if you want to.

2

Holding each half shell carefully
pierce a hole in the top with your
needle. Ask a grown-up to help.

3

Thread a length of wool through the
hole and knot on the inside of the
shell. Tie to a branch.

15

Nest cakes

What you will need

To make 6 cakes

★ 4 tablespoons golden syrup
★ 150 g margarine or butter
★ 50 g cocoa powder
★ 150 g shredded wheat
★ small sweet eggs

- saucepan
- wooden spoon
- greased baking tray
- bowl

1

Put the first three ingredients into a saucepan. Ask a grown-up to stir them, over a low heat, until melted.

2

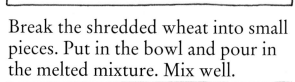

Break the shredded wheat into small pieces. Put in the bowl and pour in the melted mixture. Mix well.

3

Place small amounts on a greased baking tray. Mould into nest shapes. Leave to harden.

4

Arrange small sweet eggs inside the nests.

Paper boats

These boats are very simple to make. Build a whole fleet and have races with your friends. You can personalize them with names and coloured flags.

What you will need
- ★ double sheet of broadsheet newspaper, folded
- ★ felt-tip pens
- ★ toothpicks
- ★ coloured paper and glue

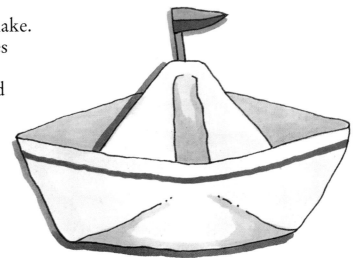

1

Fold the folded double sheet into two and fold corners down.

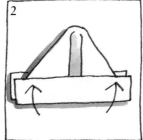

2

Fold up bottom edges.

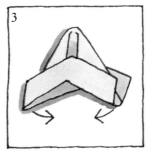

3

Bring ends together.

4

Flatten sideways.

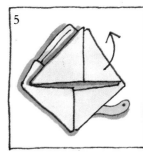

5

Turn top corner up.

6

Turn back corner up to match.

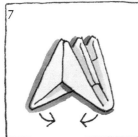

7

Bring ends together.

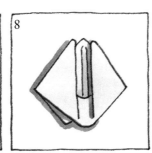

8

Flatten sideways.

9

Gently open by pulling ends down.

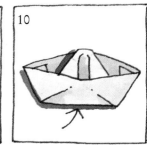

10

Open out central point from bottom.

Glue pieces of coloured paper on to toothpicks to make flags.

Decorate your boats using felt-tip pens.

Spot the difference

Can you spot ten differences between these two pictures?

18

Butterfly clip

What you will need
- ★ thick coloured paper
- ★ pencil
- ★ scissors
- ★ sticky shapes
- ★ glue
- ★ sequins
- ★ scraps of coloured paper
- ★ clothes' peg

1

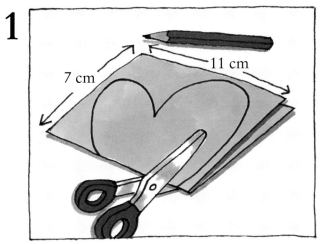

7 cm

11 cm

Fold thick paper in half. Draw and then cut out wing shapes.

2

Decorate both sides with sticky shapes or glue on sequins and cut or torn coloured paper shapes.

3

Cut two thin strips of thick paper 7 cm long. Ask a grown-up to help you curl them along the edge of scissors. Glue on to closed end of peg.

4

Just glue along centre of wings.

Glue butterfly wings on peg below antennae. Clip on to the edges of lampshades or use it to keep your wellies together.

Modelling marzipan

Fruits

These pretty fruits can be used to decorate cakes or be given as presents in small baskets (see centre pages) or boxes. Make delicious home-made marzipan or you can use bought marzipan – white is best if you want to colour it.

What you will need

★ 100 g ground almonds
★ 100 g mixed caster and icing sugar
★ 2 tsp lemon juice
★ egg white

• bowl
• spoon
• plastic bag

Roll marzipan strawberries in caster sugar.

Mould into fruit shapes and paint with food colouring.

Use cloves for stalks, eyes and nose (but don't eat them).

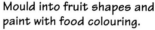

1 Mix the ground almonds, sugars and lemon juice in the bowl.

2 Add a very small amount of egg white and mix thoroughly until the paste is very stiff.

3 Marzipan will keep in the fridge for up to 4 weeks.

Knead paste on a surface dusted with icing sugar. Keep in a plastic bag until you want to use it.

Chick

What you will need
★ home-made or bought white marzipan
★ yellow and red food colouring and paintbrush
★ 2 cloves

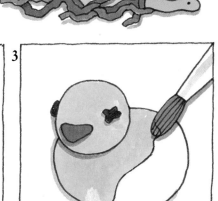

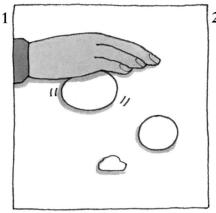

1	2	3

Roll the marzipan into two balls – one larger than the other. Keep a tiny bit aside.

Push the smaller ball on top of the other. Form the left-over piece into a beak and put in place.

Paint the chick yellow. When dry paint the beak red and push cloves in for eyes.

Rabbit

What you will need
★ home-made or bought white marzipan
★ blue food colouring and paintbrush
★ 3 cloves

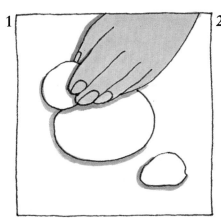

Roll the marzipan into two balls – one larger than the other. Keep a tiny bit aside.

Push the smaller ball on top of the other. Form the left-over piece into a tail and two ears.

Paint the rabbit blue, leaving the tail white. Push cloves in for eyes and nose.

Frog bean bag

Make one frog to sit on a shelf or three to juggle with. Vary the patterns and colours of the fabric.

Before you begin
• get a grown-up to help you iron out creases in the fabric.

What you will need
★ tracing paper and pencil
★ patterned fabric
★ scissors and pins
★ needle and thread
★ paintbrush
★ dried beans
★ small piece of felt
★ glue (if you want)

1

Ask a grown-up to help you cut it out carefully.

Trace frog template (on opposite page) on to tracing paper and pin on to two layers of fabric.

2

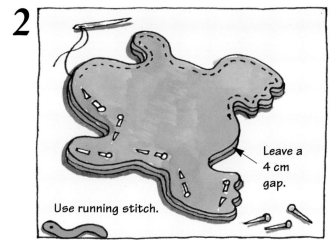

Leave a 4 cm gap.

Use running stitch.

Remove tracing paper and pin fabric together with patterned sides facing inwards. Sew 1 cm in from edge.

3

Turn inside out, pushing into corners with the end of the paintbrush. Fill with beans until full but floppy.

4

Sew up gap very firmly. Cut out small felt circles for the eyes and glue or sew them on.

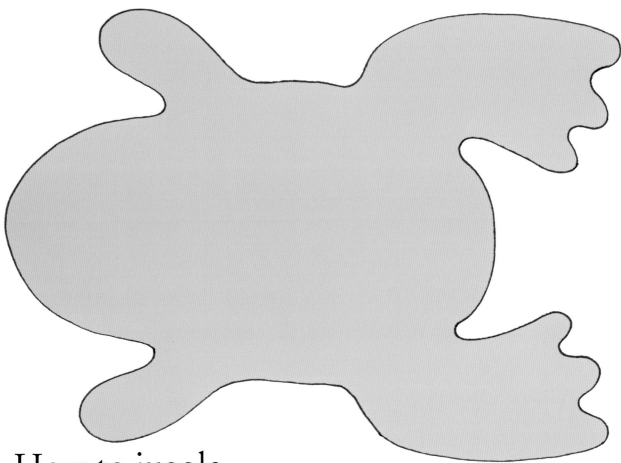

How to juggle

Juggling takes practice but it's great fun. Stand relaxed with your elbows near your body and your hands at waist height.

Hold balls or frog bags in the palm of your hands. Use a scooping movement as you throw.

Try throwing two balls to and fro to begin with, throwing up in an arc. Don't throw the second ball until the first has started to come down.

Now try with three balls or bags.

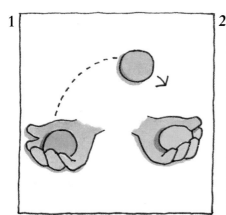

Throw one of the bags (from the two bag hand) up into an arc over to the (one bag) hand.

As the first bag begins to fall throw the bag held in the receiving hand in an arc, to the other hand.

As this bag starts to fall throw the third bag up and so on.

Easter weather

Spring, and therefore Easter, is a time of varied weather. Because Easter can be as much as a month apart from one year to the next there might be snow one year and sunshine the next.

Long before modern weather forecasts, people looked at the sky, trees and the way birds and animals behaved to see what the weather would be like.

See if these old sayings are true.

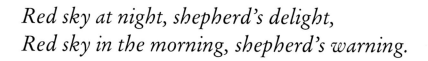

Red sky at night, shepherd's delight,
Red sky in the morning, shepherd's warning.

Rain in the night,
Next day will be bright.

Rain before seven,
Fine before eleven.

If the rooks build high the weather will be dry.

When the stars begin to muddle,
The earth will soon become a puddle.

SUMMER

- Always take great care with sharp tools such as scissors, needles and knives.
- Always cover work surfaces with newspaper before you start to paint or varnish your work.
- When using a craft knife always cut away from hands. Use thick card or something similar under whatever you are cutting. Cut slowly and lightly several times.

 This symbol is to remind you to take care.

- Wash your hands and wear an apron before preparing food.

Some basic tools and materials:
paint and brushes
varnish
glue
scissors and craft knife
paper and card
coloured pencils and felt-tip pens

 This butterfly will be fluttering through the pages with you. See if you can spot it each time.

Matchbox chest

Make this chest to keep a collection of small things: beads, seeds, pins, and so on.

What you will need

★ 6 matchboxes
★ glue and sticky tape
★ plain or patterned paper
★ 6 beads
★ thin wire

1	2	3 Push 5 cm wire through bead and through front of 'drawer'.
		 Twist ends together and secure with sticky tape.
Stick the matchboxes together using the glue.	Cover the top, back and sides with the paper of your choice.	Make handles with beads and wire for the fronts of matchboxes.

 # Collecting and storing

Look out for pretty stones, shells, feathers and seeds when you are out for a walk or on the beach.

They can all be used for making the holiday picture on page 13. You could also use the shells you find to make the shell box on page 22.

When you have collected quite a few things they also look nice displayed in jars and boxes.

Stick boxes together on their sides to make a large 'display case' with lots of compartments.

Fill a glass jar or bottle with attractive, clean stones and cover with water. Top up water as it slowly evaporates.

You can paint the boxes all one colour or different colours; then leave to dry before sticking on your bits and pieces.

Old buttons look good arranged together.

Pleated paper fans

What you will need
★ paper (see below)
★ card
★ sticky tape
★ scissors
★ paint, brushes and glitter
  (if you want)

Decorating your fans
Here are some ideas:
• Use coloured paper or patterned paper, like wallpaper samples or old gift wrap.
• Cut a lacy pattern in plain white paper (see opposite).
  • Lay the finished fan on newspaper and flick paint on it with a brush.
  • Paint thick lines along the shape of the open fan using different colours.
  • Sprinkle glitter on the wet paint.

1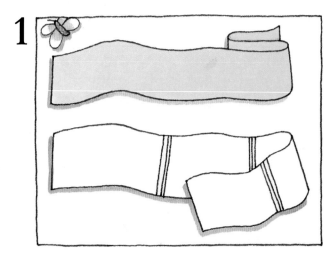

Cut a strip of paper 152 cm long and 18 cm wide - you can join pieces of paper together.

2

Start at one end and fold the paper up into 2 cm wide pleats.

3

Just cut a few pleats at a time.

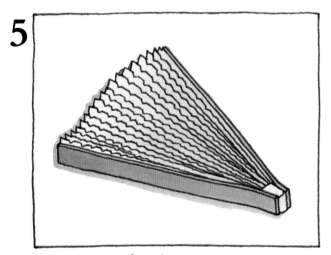

For a lacy fan cut out small pieces along one or both sides of the pleats.

4

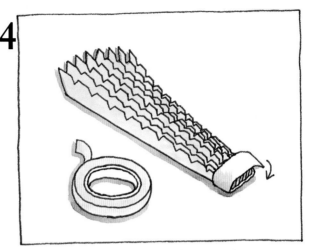

Bind one end of the folded fan firmly with sticky tape.

5

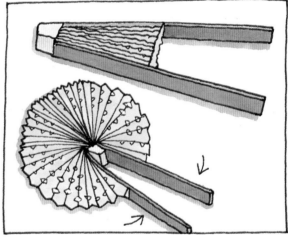

Cut two card strips 2 cm x 18 cm and stick along the outer edges of fan. Open the fan out.

For a circular fan cut two card strips 2 cm x 30 cm and stick along the outer edges of fan, but not covering the sticky tape.   Open fan.

Lemonade

What you will need

To make 1.2 litres
★ 4 lemons
★ 75 g caster sugar
★ 1.2 litres water
★ lemon squeezer and sharp knife
★ jug
★ saucepan and wooden spoon

1

Cut the lemons in half and squeeze. Pour the juice into the jug.

Rub lemon around a glass rim and dip in sugar.

2

Ask a grown-up to help you melt the sugar in the water. Stir over a low heat until dissolved.

3

Add this syrup to the lemon juice. Stir and cool in fridge. Serve with ice.

Ice lollies

What you will need
* ★ diluted squash or fruit juice
* ★ fruit pieces (if you want)
* ★ moulds or old yoghurt pots
* ★ lolly sticks
* ★ tin foil
* ★ tray or freezer-proof dish

You can also make 'mini' lollies in an ice tray with toothpicks or add fruity ice cubes to fruit drinks. Cut the ends off the toothpicks.

1 Twist centre of strip around stick and bend ends over rim of moulds.

Hold the stick in place and keep upright in mould using a twisted strip of tin foil. Place on the tray.

2

If you want to put in pieces of fruit such as orange, strawberry, melon or grape, do so now, carefully.

3

Pour in the fruit juice up to the rim. Place the tray carefully in the freezer. Leave until frozen.

Visor

What you will need
★ thin card
★ tracing paper
★ soft pencil
★ craft knife and scissors
★ sticky tape
★ paint and brushes or pens and decorations of your choice

1

Trace the template on the page opposite (including the dotted line) using tracing paper and pencil.

2

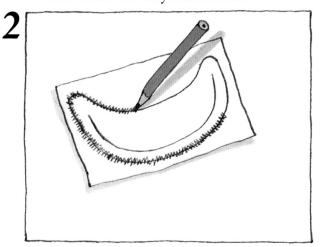

Turn over the tracing paper and scribble over lines with the soft pencil.

3

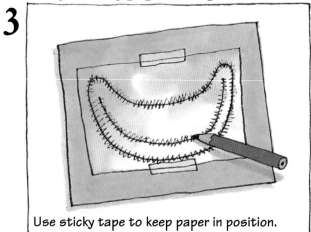

Use sticky tape to keep paper in position.

Turn over and retrace along lines onto thin card. Cut out inner line with knife and outside with scissors.

8

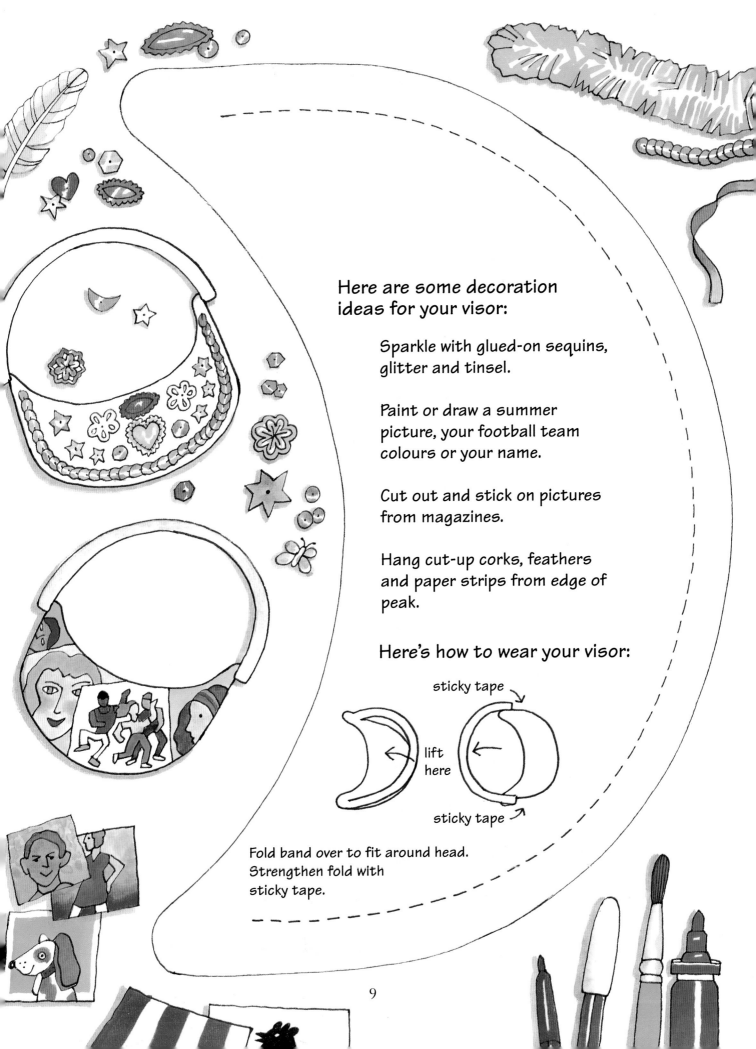

Here are some decoration ideas for your visor:

Sparkle with glued-on sequins, glitter and tinsel.

Paint or draw a summer picture, your football team colours or your name.

Cut out and stick on pictures from magazines.

Hang cut-up corks, feathers and paper strips from edge of peak.

Here's how to wear your visor:

sticky tape

lift here

sticky tape

Fold band over to fit around head. Strengthen fold with sticky tape.

9

Summer jewellery

Here are some ideas for making wonderful, funky summer jewellery for yourself, or as gifts for your family and friends. Have lots of fun collecting:

seeds

pasta shapes

corks

shells and stones
(with holes)

Before you begin
- Cover your work surface.
- Take care when you use a craft knife or needle.
- Check the length of the necklace or bracelet.

You could start with this simple necklace.

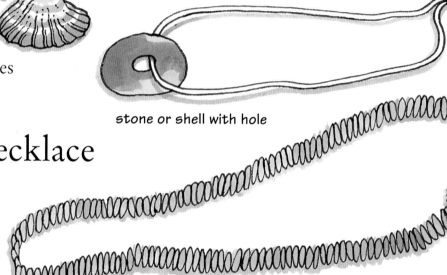

string or leather thong

stone or shell with hole

Melon-seed necklace

What you will need
★ melon
★ thread
★ sieve and kitchen paper
★ sharp needle
★ paint and brush (if you want)

1

Scoop out the melon seeds. Wash in the sieve, removing bits of melon.

2

Lay the seeds out on kitchen paper to dry thoroughly.

3 Paint seeds if you like.

Using the sharp needle thread seeds onto thread. Tie ends together.

Cork bracelet

What you will need

★ corks and beads
★ paint, varnish and brushes
★ large needle and thin elastic
★ craft knife

1 Ask a grown-up to help cut each cork into four pieces.

2 Paint the corks in bright colours and leave to dry. Varnish.

3 Thread onto elastic with needle alternating with beads. Tie ends together.

Pasta brooch

What you will need

★ thick card and scissors
★ pasta shapes
★ glue, paint, brushes, varnish
★ safety-pin and sticky tape

1 This could be any shape you like.

Cut out the card shape.

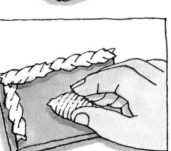

2 Arrange and glue on the pasta shapes you have selected.

Paint if you like.

3 When dry, turn it over and tape on the safety-pin. Varnish.

Souvenir scrap book

Make a simple scrap book with souvenirs of your holiday. If you go away or stay at home collect lots of 'scraps', like photos, stamps, coins, wrappers and tickets.

What you will need

★ 1 sheet of thin card
★ sheets of plain paper for pages
★ needle and wool or ribbon
★ scissors and glue

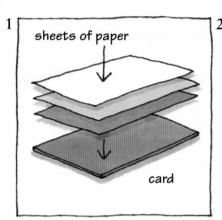

1 sheets of paper

card

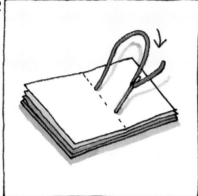

2

3

Make sure the sheets of paper and card are all the same size. Place paper on top of card. Fold it all in two.

Open and sew together along central crease with needle and wool.

Tie the two ends together tightly in a bow.

Holiday picture

Make a special collage picture of your best souvenirs from your holiday or a day out. Here's how you can frame them. They'll remind you of summer all through the year!

What you will need
★ corrugated card
★ craft knife
★ glue
★ pencil and ruler

1

Cut two pieces of card the same size.

2

Cut out a hole inside one piece of card to make a frame.

3

Glue the frame piece on top of other piece of card. Decorate the frame.

Collect autographs of people you meet, take their photographs.

Decorate the frame with paint or glue pictures onto it - you could cover it with maps.

Pot pourri

You can vary the flowers and herbs you use to achieve different smells. Try a mixture of lavender, honeysuckle and lemon balm. Concentrated flower oils are available from most chemists.

What you will need
- ★ scented rose petals
- ★ scented flowers and herbs
- ★ 1 orange and 1 lemon
- ★ 1 tablespoon mixed spice
- ★ concentrated lavender or rose oil
- ★ paper and baking tray
- ★ grater and large bowl
- ★ jar with screw lid

1

Pull off petals and dry on paper away from sunlight. Turn over twice a day until completely dry.

2

Grate the lemon and orange peel onto a baking tray and ask a grown-up to put it into a low oven to dry.

3

Put the dried peel in the large bowl and add petals, mixed spice and a few drops of flower oil. Mix well.

4

Store in the jar with the lid on. Put into a pretty bowl to make your room smell nice.

Rose-water

You can use this in the bath, and to cool your face and hands.

What you will need
- ★ 2 handfuls of scented rose petals
- ★ 225 g sugar
- ★ 1.2 litres water
- ★ large bowl
- ★ saucepan and wooden spoon
- ★ sieve and clean jars with lids

1 Pull the petals carefully off the stalks and put into a large bowl.

2 With the help of a grown-up slowly dissolve the sugar in the water, stirring over a low heat.

3 Pour over the rose petals and leave for 1 hour. Stir thoroughly and leave for another hour.

You could make pretty labels and stick them on the jars.

4 Strain and pour into the jars. The rose-water will last for about a week, kept in the fridge.

Fun on the beach

Can you spot ten differences between these two pictures?

When you are out, walking or playing, collect interesting shaped stones. Choose big, smooth ones that you can paint pictures on like the ones shown below.

What you will need

★ large smooth stones
★ thick paint and brushes
★ varnish
★ pencil

Wash the stones and leave them to dry. Decide what you are going to paint on your stone and start by painting the base colour all over. Draw out details with pencil when dry, and then paint, leaving each colour to dry before adding the next. Varnish.

Super jet

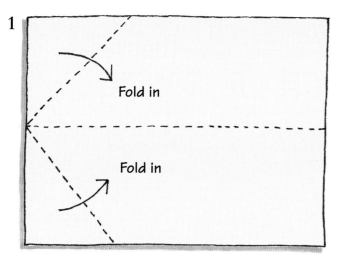

Make a few of these paper aeroplanes and give them to your friends. You could have races!
Follow the dotted lines as carefully as you can when folding.

1

Fold in

Fold in

Fold paper in half lengthways. Open and fold corners down at one end.

What you will need
★ A4 sheets of plain or coloured paper
★ felt-tip pens or coloured pencils and decorations of your choice.

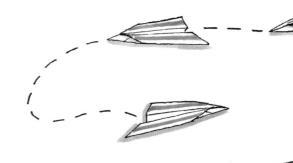

2

A
Fold in

Fold in
B

Fold down sides, making sure points A and B meet in centre.

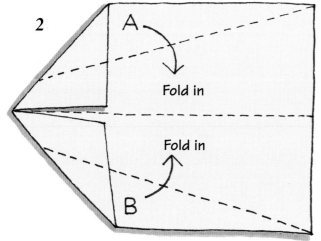

3

C
Fold in

Fold in
D

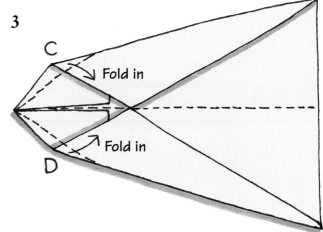

Fold in points C and D, making sure these meet in centre. Turn the plane over carefully.

4

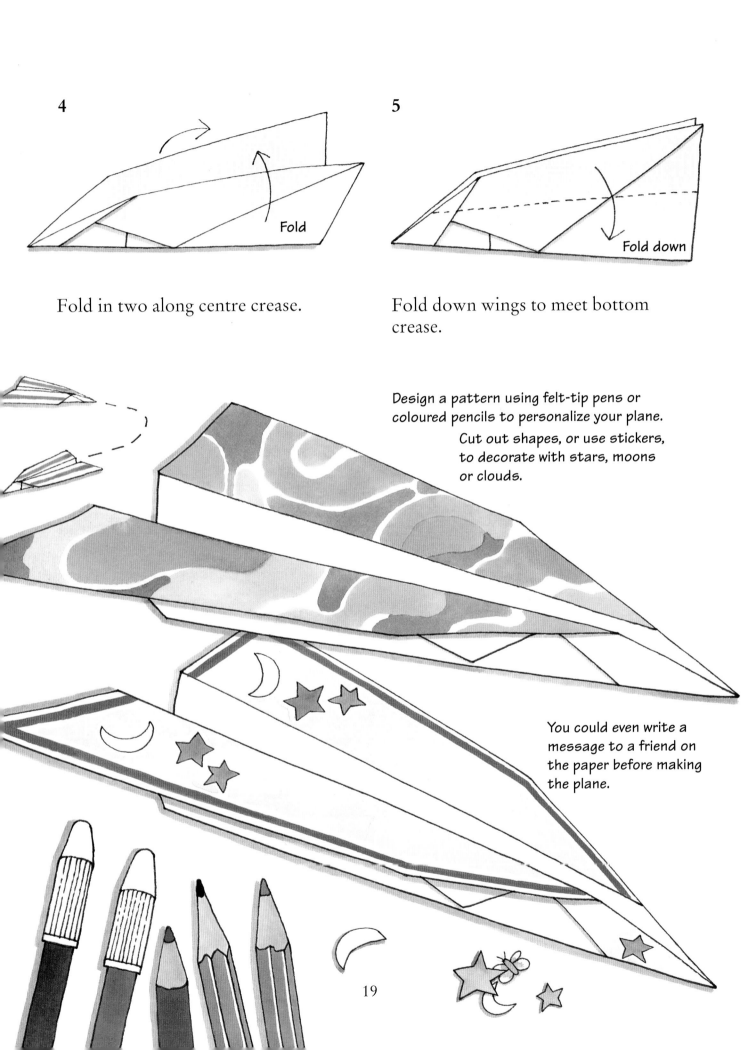

Fold in two along centre crease.

5

Fold down wings to meet bottom crease.

Design a pattern using felt-tip pens or coloured pencils to personalize your plane.

Cut out shapes, or use stickers, to decorate with stars, moons or clouds.

You could even write a message to a friend on the paper before making the plane.

19

Decorating ice-cream

It's great fun decorating ice-cream with delicious sweets and sauces.

What you will need
★ wafers and cones
★ fruit and nuts
★ cake decorations
★ sweets and sponge fingers

Butterscotch sauce

50 g butter
4 level tablespoons brown sugar
2 level tablespoons golden syrup
Ask a grown-up to help you melt all the ingredients in a saucepan over a low heat. Boil for 1 minute.

Chocolate sauce

75 g caster sugar
75 g brown sugar
75 g cocoa powder
300 ml milk
1 teaspoon vanilla essence
25 g butter

Ask a grown-up to help you and put all ingredients in a saucepan over a low heat. Stir until sugar has dissolved. Slowly bring to the boil. Boil without stirring for 5 minutes.

Knickerbocker glory
Put layers of ice-cream, fruit and sauce into a tall glass and decorate top.

Ice-cream boat
Cut a wafer into two triangles and stick into a dollop of ice-cream in a sauce sea.

Face cornets
Make faces with sweets – pour a little sauce on top and sprinkle with nuts or cake decorations. Make ears of sponge fingers.

Matching pairs

Can you find the matching pairs in each row?

Shell box

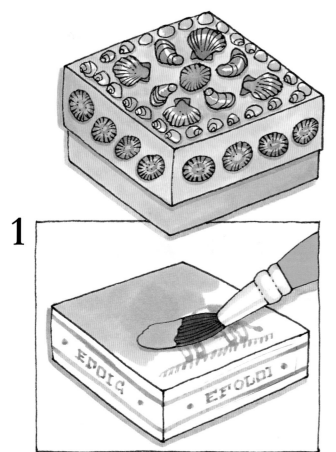

What you will need
★ shells
★ box with lid
★ varnish
★ glue and glue brush
★ thick paint and brush

Before you begin
• Plan your shells, making sure you have enough to cover the box lid and create your own design.
• You can make a regular or random design as shown below.

1

Paint the box all over covering any lettering or pictures. Leave to dry.

2   Start in the centre of the box.

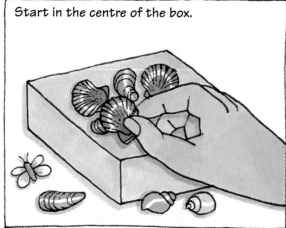

Put a dab of glue on each shell and press firmly into position onto the lid of the box.

3

Stick shells around the edge of the box if liked. When dry brush shells with varnish.

22

Sand sculptures

- Create your own sculptures in a sandpit or on the beach. Make a monster, funny faces or a car, boat or rocket.
- Get your friends to help and make something really big!
- Using damp sand, make different shapes with washed yoghurt and mousse pots. Form the large shapes with your hands - patting down the sand firmly.

- Make patterns with a stick or by pressing in the rims or bottoms of pots.
- Decorate with anything you can find. Seaweed and leaves make wonderful hair. Make faces or interesting patterns with feathers, stones, shells and sticks.

Use a paper plate for a steering wheel.

Finish off your monster/dinosaur with a row of small sandcastles, with pointed shells and grasses, along its back.

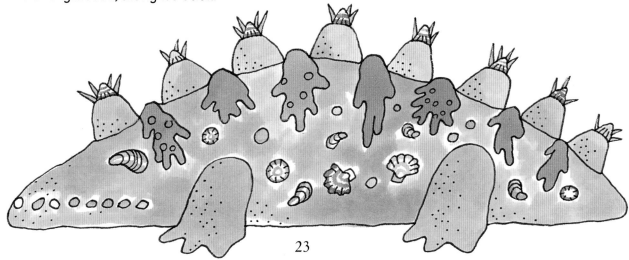

Here are two simple games you can play with pebbles or stones. Wash the stones if necessary.

Stone circle

(for two players)

You could play this game inside or out.

- Put 15 stones in a circle and decide who starts.
- The first player picks up a number of stones – either one, two or three.
- The other player does the same.
- Take turns until there are no stones left.
- The winner is the player who has an odd number of stones.

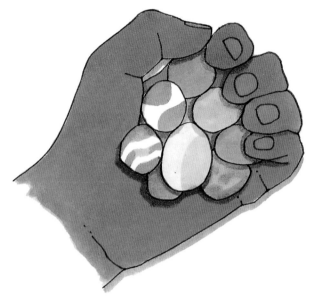

Hands full

Play this with any number of friends - but make sure you all have about the same size hands!

The aim of this game is to see who can hold the most stones in one hand. You could play it inside or out.

- Collect a heap of stones or pebbles.
- Take turns to pick them up, one by one, with one hand and hold them in the other.
- Use the same heap of stones for each player.

AUTUMN

Before you begin

- Always take great care with sharp tools such as scissors, needles and knives.
- Always cover work surfaces with newspaper before you start to paint or varnish your work.
- When using a craft knife always cut away from hands. Use thick card or something similar under whatever you are cutting. Cut slowly and lightly several times.
- Wash your hands and wear an apron before preparing food.

Some basic tools and materials:
paint and brushes
varnish
glue
scissors and craft knife
paper and card
coloured pencils and felt-tip pens

 This symbol is to remind you to take care.

An acorn has fallen on to each page. See if you can spot it as you go through the book.

See if you can find ...

berries, hips and haws (see page 20)

fir cones – some on twigs

acorns

autumn leaves on small branches

interesting twigs

autumn leaves

seeds

crab (wild) apples and windfalls

wild mushrooms (fungi)

conkers

nuts

Collecting and storing

Make sure everything you want to keep is dry and free from insects.

Keep pretty twigs and flower seeds hung upside down or in a vase.

You can frame pressed leaves (see page 22) and write their name underneath.

Keep fir cones, acorns, nuts, conkers and twigs in labelled shoe boxes.

Keep a scrapbook of pressed leaves (see page 22) and name each one.

Keep seeds in little packets.

Plastic or glass jars are useful for storage.

Glue shallow boxes together and display your collections.

Leaf pictures

Leaves come in all shapes and sizes. Collect a good selection and use them in these projects. Make pictures or decorate wrapping paper and writing paper and envelopes. Use autumnal colours of yellow, red and orange.

Before you begin
• Cover your work surface.

Splatter leaf picture

What you will need
★ leaves
★ paper
★ coins
★ glue
★ old toothbrush
★ poster paints
★ black paper and scissors

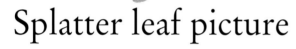

1 Place a leaf on some paper, and put a coin on top to prevent it moving.

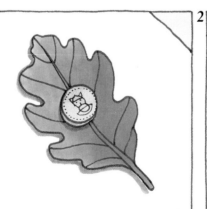

2 Hold toothbrush about 10 cm from the leaf.

Dip the toothbrush in thickish paint. Run finger along bristles to splatter paint around edge of leaf.

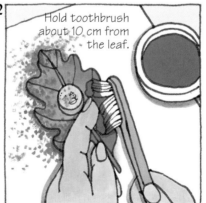

3 Cut vase or basket in black paper and glue below leaves.

Remove the leaf. When the paint is dry, add more leaves and splatter in the same way.

4

Leaf print

What you will need

★ poster paints and brush
★ leaves
★ paper
★ newspaper

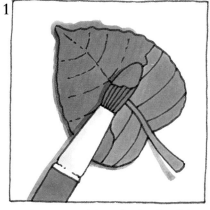

Paint one side of a leaf with thickish paint.

Use folded newspaper and press down firmly.

Turn the leaf over and position it on paper. Place newspaper on top.

Remove the newspaper and leaf. When dry add many more leaf prints.

Leaf rubbing

What you will need

★ thin paper
★ leaves
★ wax crayons or soft, coloured pencils

Place paper over a leaf (where you want the rubbing to appear).

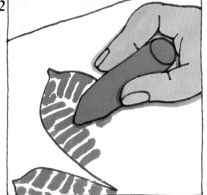

Rub the paper firmly over the leaf with a crayon. Go carefully over veins and edges.

Add more rubbings to make a pretty design.

Odd one out

Each of these fungi has a pair – except one.
Can you spot the odd one out?

Baked apples

Apples are plentiful at this time of year and make delicious puddings.

What you will need
★ 4 large apples
★ 2 tablespoons raisins
★ 75 g soft brown sugar
★ 1 teaspoon cinnamon
★ 60 g butter, cut into pieces
★ cream to serve

Warning! Ask a grown-up to help.

1

Wash the apples and remove the cores with a small sharp knife. Score around the middle of each apple.

2

Put the apples in an ovenproof dish. Mix the raisins, sugar, cinnamon and butter together and stuff into the holes.

3

Serve hot with cream.

Bake in a moderate oven (180°C/350°F/Gas 4) for 45 minutes to an hour. Baste occasionally.

Another filling
1 tablespoon golden syrup
1/2 teaspoon grated lemon rind (or 1 tablespoon chopped nuts)
25 g butter
3 tablespoons warm water.

Fir cones

You will find these under fir trees. Different-shaped cones fall from different types of tree. Some will be attached to twigs. Collect a good variety of undamaged cones.

What you will need
★ different-shaped fir cones
★ glue and scissors
★ paper, card, feathers, beads and small sticks, paper and string
★ thin wire
★ white and gold or silver paint

Animals and birds

The size and shape of the cones will help you decide what creature to make. Here are some ideas.

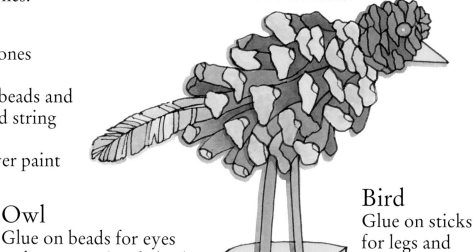

Owl
Glue on beads for eyes and a paper triangle beak.

Bird
Glue on sticks for legs and large card feet, a feather tail, bead eyes and a card triangle beak.

Mouse
Glue on bead eyes, rounded card ears and a string tail.

Candle decoration
Colour with a little silver or gold paint. Wire together in a circle. Place a candle in the centre.

Fir tree
Use an open cone (they open in the warmth). Colour with a little white paint for snow. Glue the bottom of the cone on to a section of painted card tube.

Popcorn

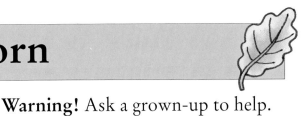

What you will need

- ★ 1 tablespoon sunflower oil
- ★ thick-based saucepan with lid
- ★ 50-75 g popcorn
- ★ 25 g butter
- ★ small saucepan for melting butter
- ★ wooden spoon
- ★ shake of salt or sugar

Warning! Ask a grown-up to help.

1

Heat the oil in the saucepan. When hot, pour in enough popcorn to cover the base.

2

Hold the lid firmly on the saucepan and shake continuously over medium heat until the popping stops.

3

Remove the popcorn from the heat. Melt the butter and stir into the popcorn. Add salt or sugar.

Paper cones

What you will need

- ★ coloured paper
- ★ scissors
- ★ felt-tip pens or crayons
- ★ sticky tape

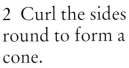

2 Curl the sides round to form a cone.

3 Tape together. Make sure no hole is left at the bottom.

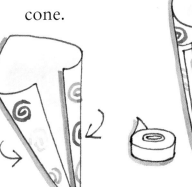

1 Cut the paper into 22 cm squares and decorate.

Hibernation and migration

As the weather gets colder and food scarcer, some creatures hide away and go into a deep sleep called 'hibernation'. During the autumn they prepare themselves by eating a lot to put on fat for the long winter sleep.

Hedgehogs curl up tight and bury themselves in nests of dry leaves. Always check for hedgehogs before lighting a bonfire!

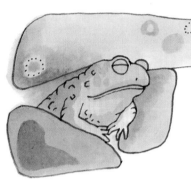

Frogs and toads hide away under old logs or in stone walls. Male frogs prefer the bottom of a pond.

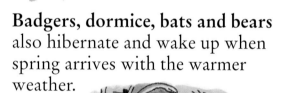

Badgers, dormice, bats and bears also hibernate and wake up when spring arrives with the warmer weather.

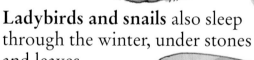

Ladybirds and snails also sleep through the winter, under stones and leaves.

Squirrels and mice don't hibernate but they prepare for winter by gathering and storing food. They become less active and rather dozy.

In the autumn and winter, some birds move or **migrate** from one country to another. Swifts, swallows and martins are amongst the many species which fly from the cold of northern Europe to the warmth of Africa. They return in the spring.

Feeding the birds

Towards the end of autumn, the weather gets colder and the earth freezes. Berries and insects disappear. Birds that don't migrate (see page 10) need some help with their diet until the spring. As well as pleasing the birds, you can enjoy watching them from the window.

What you will need
★ porridge oats
★ birdseed and nuts
★ brown breadcrumbs
★ cooked rice and grated cheese
★ lard
★ bowl, wooden spoon, small saucepan
★ holder for the mixture and string

1

Mix all the ingredients, except the lard, together in a large bowl.

2

Warning! Ask a grown-up to help.

Add enough lard to bind everything together.

Melt some lard slowly in a saucepan. Pour it over the mixture in the bowl and stir together thoroughly.

3

Tie string firmly around fir cone.

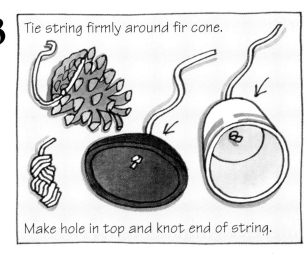

Make hole in top and knot end of string.

To hold the mixture, use old yoghurt pots, half coconut shells or large open fir cones. Hang them up with the string.

4

Hang from a branch or bird table.

Fill the pots or coconut shells with the mixture. Push it down firmly. Coat the fir cone. Leave to harden.

Autumn customs around the world

Autumn is the third season of the year. In Europe and North America, September, October and November are the autumn months. But in Australia and New Zealand autumn is in March, April and May. In autumn, crops, fruits and berries ripen and are gathered before the winter. So this is the time when people prepare for the long nights of winter and bring in the harvest.

Harvest Festival is one of the most important Christian occasions. Churches are decorated with sheaves of corn, fruit, vegetables and flowers. People give thanks for the crops and often have a special supper to celebrate.

Corn dollies are traditional plaited straw shapes used in the Christian harvest festivities. They were taken into church and hung up in barns.

In Japan, people give thanks for the rice harvest at the **New Taste Festival** in November and have a holiday.

In November in the USA **Thanksgiving Day** is a national festival to give thanks for peace and plenty. It was started in 1621 by a group of settlers from England after their first good harvest in their new country. People eat a special dinner of turkey, cranberry sauce, sweet potatoes and pumpkin pie.

Diwali, a Festival of Lights, is one of the most important festivals in the Hindu calendar held in late October or early November. People remember the story of Ram, a favourite Hindu god. They light lamps outside people's houses and have parties with family and friends and give presents and sweets.

In September to celebrate the rice harvest, the Chinese have a **Moon Festival**. They have a procession of lanterns with candles and a feast of traditional foods like little rice cakes shaped like moons.

On November 5th, people in Britain celebrate **Guy Fawkes Night**. Guy Fawkes tried to blow up the Houses of Parliament in 1605. People light bonfires, burn 'guys' (dummies made of rags) and let off fireworks.

All over Scandinavia, people go to **Autumn Markets** which sell local produce and items for Christmas. They can also buy reindeer meat, fish and pine furniture. In southern Sweden in Skane, families and friends celebrate **Marten Gas** (Goose Day) with a feast of black soup, made of goose blood, and roast goose.

Conkers are the fruit of the horse chestnut tree and are used in a popular game by boys and girls in Britain. The conkers are threaded on to a string and players take it in turns to hit each other's conker until one is broken.

13

Jar labels

Hand-made labels make a lovely finish to home-made jam and chutney or bottled fruit and vegetables. Give them to friends and family or make them for a school or church bazaar.

What you will need

★ paper
★ pencil and ruler
★ glue and scissors
★ felt-tip pens and crayons

Round or cut off the corners too.

Glue on to jars.

1 Use a ruler and pencil to divide the paper into rectangles, 8 cm x 3.5 cm.

2 Cut carefully along the pencil lines with scissors.

3 Colour a border and decorate with small pictures of fruit. Leave space for the name and date.

Cover the jar lids with pretty fabric and tie with ribbon or coloured tape.

QUIN

PLUM JAM September

Tomato Chutney

ROSE HIP JELLY

YELLOW TOMATOES October

Write the type of jam or fruit and the date.

Seed and bean frame

What you will need

★ old cardboard boxes
★ ruler and pencil
★ craft knife
★ sticky tape and glue
★ string

★ selection of beans and seeds

Warning! Take care when using a craft knife (see page 2 for help).

Cut 2 equal size pieces of cardboard. Draw a rectangle in the centre of one and cut it out (with grown-up help).

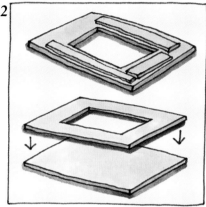

Cut 3 strips of cardboard and glue around 3 sides of the hole. Turn over and glue on to the second piece.

Gap to slide in picture.

Tape a loop of string on the back, just below the top edge.

4 Draw out a simple design on the frame and start to glue on the beans and seeds. Continue until completely covered.

sunflower seeds

yellow split peas

mung beans

rice

red kidney beans

green lentils

poppy seeds

Nuts

Nuts ripen in autumn. How many different ones can you spot in the shops?

hazelnut

brazil nut

peanut

walnut

Walnut shell halves

Tortoise

Glue shell on to paper. Bend limbs and head.

Place a shell on paper and draw round it. Add legs, a head and tail. Cut out.

Basket

Fill with tiny things.

Cut out a coloured paper strip about 6 cm long. Glue the ends inside a shell.

Bird

Hang up with thread attached to top.

Draw a long bird body on coloured paper and cut it out. Glue a shell in the middle.

Boat

Cut off toothpick end.

Cut a small square of paper and thread it on to a toothpick. Push it into a tiny piece of Plasticine.

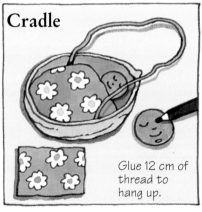

Cradle

Glue 12 cm of thread to hang up.

Draw a face on a large wooden bead. Glue it in a shell. Fold and glue a small piece of material as a blanket.

Decoration

Thread a bead on 20 cm of silk thread. Place at the bottom of a shell. Knot the top and glue on to another half.

Nut nibbles

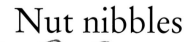

Brazil nuts dipped in melted chocolate.

Brazil nuts wrapped in marzipan.

String of peanuts to hang up for the birds.

16

Warning!
Some people are allergic to nuts. If in doubt, don't eat them.

Spot the difference

Can you spot ten differences between these two pictures?

17

Salt dough magnets

These salt dough shapes have been left the rough brown dough colour. But if you like, you can paint or varnish them after cooking. Ask a grown-up to help with the oven.

What you will need

★ 100 g plain flour
★ 50 g salt
★ 1 teaspoon cooking oil
★ 80 ml water
★ mixing bowl
★ wooden spoon
★ fork, wooden skewer, blunt knife
★ greased baking tray
★ small magnets and glue

1

Sift the flour and salt into the mixing bowl and add the oil. Add water a little at a time and mix until smooth.

2

Place the dough on a floured surface. Knead well and form into shapes.

3

Add details – hedgehog spines with a fork, eyes with a wooden skewer, leaf veins with a knife.

4

Place on a greased baking tray. Put in the oven overnight on the lowest setting. Take out and leave to cool. Glue magnets on to the backs.

Cheese scones

Delicious eaten warm with butter.

What you will need – *for 12 scones*
★ 225 g self-raising flour
★ pinch of salt
★ 1 level teaspoon baking powder
★ 40 g butter or margarine
★ 100 g grated Cheddar cheese
★ 1 level teaspoon mustard powder
★ 150 ml milk

And you will need this equipment
• mixing bowl
• wooden spoon
• rolling-pin
• 5 cm cutter
• greased baking sheet
• pastry brush

1
Use the tips of fingers and thumbs.

Sift the flour, salt and baking powder into a bowl. Rub in butter until the mixture looks like breadcrumbs.

2

Stir in most of the grated cheese and mustard. Add enough milk to make a dough.

3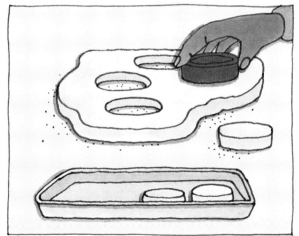

Roll the dough out on a floured surface until 2 cm thick. Cut into rounds and put on the greased baking sheet.

4
Warning! Ask a grown-up to help.

Cool on a wire rack

Brush the tops with milk and sprinkle with the remaining cheese and mustard. Bake in the oven 220°C/425°F/Gas 7 for 10 minutes or until risen and golden.

19

Berry door sign

Berries are the fruit of trees and plants and ripen in the autumn. Look in hedgerows for wild rose hips and hawthorn haws. You can make this sign with beads for berries.

What you will need

★ yellow or orange paper
★ brush and paints
★ pencil and tracing paper
★ thin card
★ scissors and glue
★ 6 red beads or varnished berries

Template

For how to use this template, see bottom of page.

1

Cut out leaves.

Splodge paint on coloured paper. When dry, draw 4 leaves with template.

2

5 cm

15 cm

Cut the sign from thin card and arrange the leaves overlapping the edges. Glue down.

3

Kate's room

Glue the beads or berries on the sign. Write the words and paint over the letters.

How to use a template

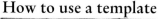

1

Trace the template shape using tracing paper and a pencil.

2

Turn over the tracing paper and scribble over the lines with a soft pencil.

3

Turn over and tape on to coloured paper. Retrace over the lines firmly.

Indoor bulbs

You can enjoy spring bulbs in winter, if you prepare them in the autumn.

What you will need
★ bulb fibre
★ water
★ bowls or jars
★ bulbs – hyacinths, daffodils, tulips and narcissi.

1

Soak all the bulb fibre in water and squeeze out excess. Half fill the bowl and arrange the bulbs on top.

2

Cover with more fibre, pressing down gently. Put in a cold dark place. Check occasionally and keep moist.

3

Bring out into the daylight when shoots appear. Continue to keep the fibre moist.

4

You can buy special glass jars or make a jam jar neck smaller with a ring of Plasticine.

Hyacinths can also be grown in glass jars. Bring out of the dark when the shoots start to grow.

Pressed leaves

Collect a variety of different leaves in perfect condition.

Place in a single layer between sheets of newspaper. Put under a pile of heavy books and leave for at least a week. Fleshy leaves will need longer.

Pressed leaf picture

What you will need
★ leaves
★ paint and brush
★ paper and glue

Keep pressed leaves flat in an envelope or folder until used.

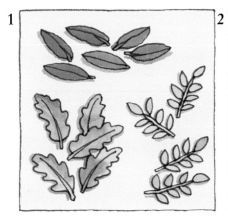

1 Pick out 3 groups of matching leaves.

2 On a large piece of paper, paint the ground and the tree trunks in black. Leave to dry.

3 Arrange the leaves as trees. Glue one at a time in position.

Light decoration

These pretty coloured leaves look lovely hanging from a light shade.

What you will need
★ paper in autumn colours
★ tracing paper and pencil
★ thread and needle
★ tissue
★ paint
★ sticky tape
★ scissors

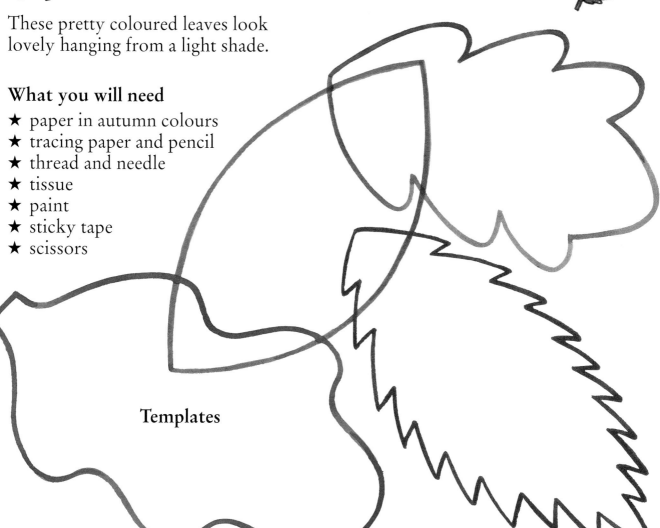

Templates

1

Dip scrunched-up tissue into a saucer of thick paint.

Trace templates (see p.20) on to coloured papers. Cut out. Add dabs of other colours using scrunched-up tissue.

2

Tie here.

Tie here.

Knot end of 40 cm length of thread. Pull through the top of one leaf. Tie the others on.

3
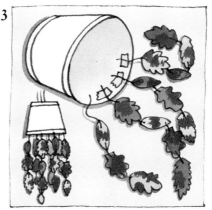

Tape the end of the thread inside a shade. Do enough to complete the circle.

Seeds

All plants have seeds. They are what new plants grow from. They come in many shapes and sizes. Some are large, such as conkers from horse chestnut trees, and some are very small like the seeds from a poppy.

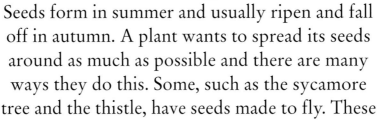

Seeds form in summer and usually ripen and fall off in autumn. A plant wants to spread its seeds around as much as possible and there are many ways they do this. Some, such as the sycamore tree and the thistle, have seeds made to fly. These get scattered by the wind. Berries, like blackberries and the wild rose hips, get eaten by birds and the seeds come out in their droppings. Squirrels and mice bury seeds like acorns.

Other seeds have hooks or prickles and stick on to the fur of animals. Then they fall off later on to the soil.

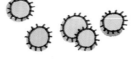

HALLOWEEN

Before you begin

- Always take great care with sharp tools such as scissors, needles and knives.
- Always cover work surfaces with newspaper before you start to paint or varnish your work.
- When using a craft knife always cut away from hands. Use thick card or something similar under whatever you are cutting. Cut slowly and lightly several times.
- Wash your hands and wear an apron before preparing food.

Some basic tools and materials:
paint and brushes
varnish
glue
scissors and craft knife
paper and card
coloured pencils and felt-tip pens

This black cat will be purring through the pages with you. See if you can spot it each time.

How to trace from templates
For some of the projects you will need to trace from templates. Here's how to do it very simply and successfully.

What you will need
★ tracing paper
★ soft pencil
★ sticky tape
★ thin card

1 Trace the template shape using the tracing paper and pencil.

2 Turn over the tracing paper and scribble over lines with the soft pencil.

3 Turn over and tape on to the thin card. Retrace over lines.

Halloween story

Halloween is a very old festival. Hundreds of years ago the Celts who lived in Britain believed that spirits of the dead and ghosts came alive to frighten them. It was known as the Festival of the Dead. **Aaaaaaaaaaaaaaaahhhh!**

When Christianity arrived in Britain a Christian festival was introduced on 1st November to replace the old Celtic one. It was called All Saints' Day or All-Hallows. But the old festival celebrated on 31st October still survived and was called All Hallows' Eve. Later the name became Hallowe'en, or Halloween.

It was a night of bonfires, games and fun. People had their fortunes told and young people played games to see who they would marry.

An Irish legend tells of Jack – a man destined to wander over the world forever with a lantern carved from a turnip. Today pumpkins make popular lanterns.

'Trick or treat' is a traditional American form of Halloween mischief. Children knock on doors and play tricks if they don't get a treat!

Aaaaaaaaaaaaaaaaahhhh!

Witch's or wizard's hat

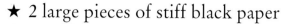

What you will need
★ 2 large pieces of stiff black paper
★ pencil
★ scissors
★ glue
★ compass
★ sticky tape

For decorating your hat
★ gold and silver stars and moons
★ glitter and glue
★ tinsel

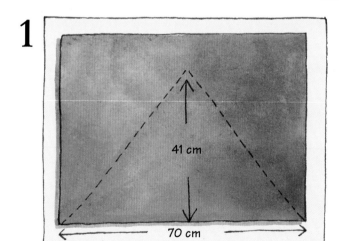

1

41 cm

70 cm

Draw a large triangle on one piece of black paper. Cut it out.

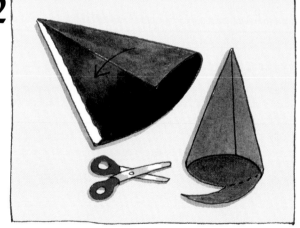

2

Put a line of glue 1 cm wide along one side of the paper. Roll paper over and stick to form cone. Cut to make bottom edge straight.

3

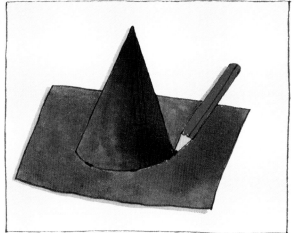

Stand the cone in the centre of the second sheet of black paper. Mark around it with the pencil.

4

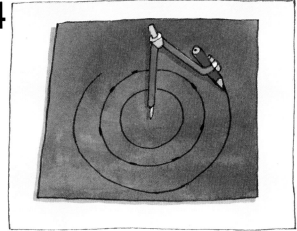

Draw a circle with the compass joining up pencil marks. Also draw an inner and outer circle as shown.

5

Cut out the outer circle. Cut a hole following inner circle. Cut a fringe inside between inner and centre circle.

6

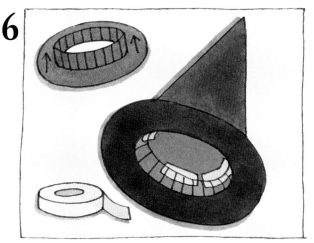

Bend fringe up. Place cone on ring with fringe inside and tape together with the sticky tape.

Witch's or wizard's hair

You can attach weird hair to your hat. Leaving a gap at the front (for your face), tape lengths of coloured wool, cut up tissue paper or plastic bags cut into fringes to the inside of the hat.

Wear a plastic witchy nose to complete the spell.

Halloween costumes

Costumes for Halloween can be made very easily and effectively with things that you probably already have at home.

Witch's cat

What you will need
- ★ close-fitting black clothes
- ★ stiff black paper
- ★ hairband
- ★ black material for tail
- ★ black thread and needle
- ★ black face paint
- ★ sticky tape
- ★ scissors

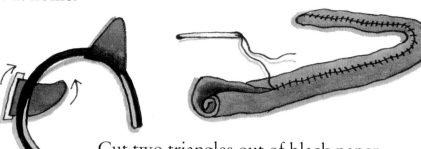

Cut two triangles out of black paper and stick to hairband. Roll black material into a sausage and sew along edge. Sew or pin on to cat's bottom. Using black face paint, draw yourself whiskers and a black nose.

Skeleton

What you will need
- ★ close-fitting black clothes
- ★ white sticky-backed plastic
- ★ white card or large white paper plate
- ★ black felt-tip pen
- ★ thin elastic
- ★ scissors

Look at the bone shapes on the right-hand centre page of the book. Draw your own (to fit the person) on the sticky-backed plastic and cut them out. Don't worry if they look a bit wobbly! Stick in position on the black clothes – this is best done when the clothes are on. Cut the paper plate or card into a skull shape and draw on the face with black pen. Make a small hole in each eye socket. Then attach the thin elastic to fit.

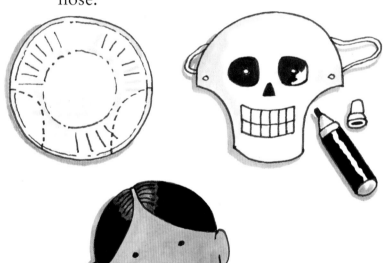

Ghost

What you will need

★ old white sheet
★ black felt-tip pen
★ black paper
★ glue
★ scissors

Drape the sheet over head. Carefully mark where the eyes are with the pen. Remove the sheet and cut two small eyeholes. Make a length of white or silver paper chain and hold or drape around neck. If necessary fasten the sheet with safety-pins on to clothed shoulders!

Shine a torch from under the sheet for an extra-special look.

Glue here

Dracula

What you will need

★ black jacket or waistcoat
★ black trousers
★ white shirt
★ black card
★ thin elastic
★ white plastic cup or yogurt pot
★ scissors
★ white and red face paint
★ hair gel

Cut a bow tie shape out of black card and attach thin elastic. Cut teeth out of white plastic cup or yogurt pot. Get dressed – paint face white with red 'blood' dribbles from corners of mouth. Put teeth into mouth and gel back hair.

Be careful to round off corners with scissors.

Witch's or wizard's cloak

1 Cut a 6 cm wide strip off a black plastic sack. Cut the sack open along side and bottom.

2 Open the sack out and cut one long edge into points.

Gather it until it is about 20 cm

3 Sew a line of running stitch near the straight edge. Tape the centre of the 6 cm strip to cloak.

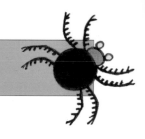

Pumpkin fun

Pumpkin lanterns

A glowing pumpkin lantern is a real must at Halloween.

What you will need

★ pumpkin (as fresh as possible)
★ sharp knife
★ metal spoon
★ dark felt-tip pen
★ night light candle

1

Ask a grown-up to help you cut off the top of the pumpkin with the sharp knife.

2

Discard the seeds and use the flesh to make soup.

Using the metal spoon scoop out the flesh. Leave a shell about 3 cm thick.

3

Draw a face on the pumpkin with the felt-tip and ask a grown-up to cut it out with the sharp knife.

Put a night light candle inside, light it, replace the lid and put the lantern in a safe place.

Try making lanterns using other squashes like marrows and make string handles for them.

Concertina pumpkins

What you will need

★ orange paper
★ scissors
★ pencil and tracing paper
★ black felt-tip pen

1

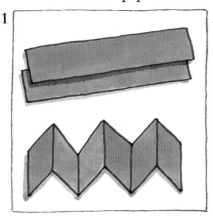

Cut the paper into 54 cm x 8 cm strips. Fold each strip like a concertina.

2 For how to trace templates see page 2.

Trace the pumpkin template from page 21 on to the top of the paper.

3 Draw on faces in black felt-tip.

Hold together and cut out, taking care to leave the paper joined on each side. Open out.

Window pumpkin

What you will need

★ orange paper
★ pencil and scissors
★ yellow tissue paper
★ sticky tape

1

Cut a pumpkin shape out of orange paper. Draw and cut out eyes, nose and mouth.

2

Cut two squares of the tissue paper big enough to cover the holes for the face.

3

Tape the tissue paper on to one side. Stick up in your window.

9

'Trick or treat' bag

When you go out 'trick or treating' you will need a bag to collect all your goodies.

What you will need
★ black plastic sack
★ scissors
★ plastic carrier bag
★ sticky tape

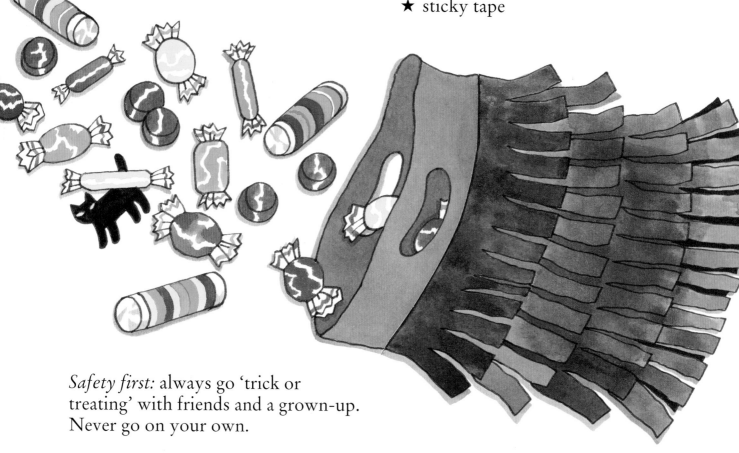

Safety first: always go 'trick or treating' with friends and a grown-up. Never go on your own.

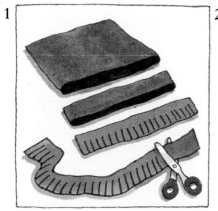

1 Cut the black plastic sack into 13 cm wide strips. Cut strips into fringes.

2 Start from bottom of bag.

With sticky tape across the top stick fringes round the carrier bag.

3 Cut off extra fringe at the edge.

Overlap each layer. Finish off just below handle.

Scary spider!

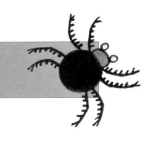

Why not make lots of these spiders and hang them all over your room and really scare your friends or your mum!

What you will need
★ black paper
★ tracing paper and pencil
★ scissors
★ sticky tape
★ thin black elastic or wool and needle
★ yellow sticky paper or paint

SPIDER TEMPLATE

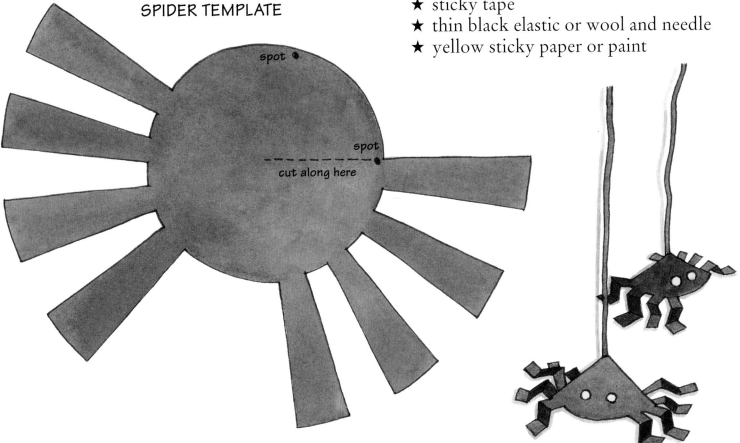

spot

spot
cut along here

1 Don't forget to mark the spots on your spider.

Follow the instructions on page 2 to trace the spider template above on to black paper. Cut it out.

2 Bend legs three times as shown.

Cut where shown and form a cone matching the spots. Fix with tape.

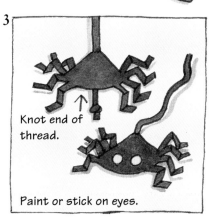

3 Knot end of thread.

Paint or stick on eyes.

Using the needle, thread a length of wool through the centre of cone. Hang up.

Broomsticks & slime

See who can climb the broomsticks and avoid slipping down the slime to reach the top first.
You will need the counters from the left-hand centre page, a die and two or more players.
Play the game like Snakes and Ladders. Take turns to throw the die and move along the squares.

Spider webs

You can make lots of these in different creepy colours! Why not make some of the spiders on page 11 to go with them?

What you will need

★ tissue paper
★ scissors
★ sticky tape

1

Fold a square of tissue paper into four. Fold once again into a triangle.

2

Cut the end opposite the point into a curve.

3

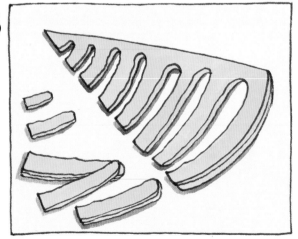

Carefully tear strips out of the paper from the one folded edge, stopping before you reach the other edge.

4

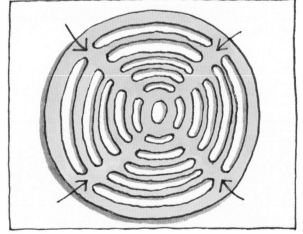

Open the web out and stick up with tape at points shown.

Fiendish faces!

Simply wear black clothes or make a cloak (see instructions on page 7) to show off these dramatic faces.

Warning – be careful not to paint too close to your eyes. Tie hair back and avoid getting face paint on clothes. Always follow printed instructions and ask a grown-up before applying hair colours.

What you will need
★ face paints
★ sponges and brushes
★ hair colours and gels

Slime

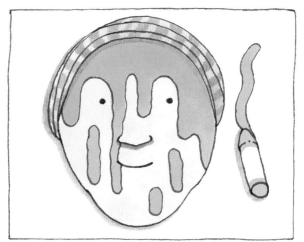

Using a sponge, colour face yellow. Draw or paint edge of slime in green. Fill in rest with a sponge.

Scarface

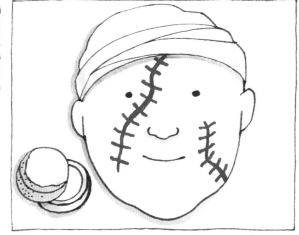

Using a sponge, colour face white. Paint on scars with a small brush and red face paint. Hide hair under a hat.

Mummy

Using a sponge, colour face white. Paint black bandage lines across face with brush.

Creepy crawly

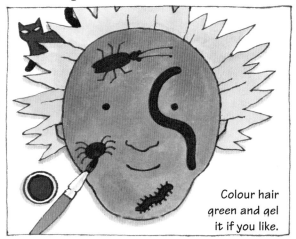

Colour hair green and gel it if you like.

Using a sponge, colour face orange. Paint on insects, worms and spiders with a small brush and black paint.

Halloween masks

Measure your face and then copy the pictures below on to card to make these exciting masks!

Spider web

Make a white card mask. Draw on a black web and hang small plastic flies and spiders from black thread.

Vampire

Cut the mask out of purple card extending the top into points. Paint black eyebrows. Dot with glue and sprinkle on glitter. Wear with vampire teeth!
(See page 7)

Night owl

Cut a fringe from a black plastic sack and stick around an orange mask. Paint on patterns in white and black. Trace beak template on to orange paper, cut out and glue on along flaps.

Beak

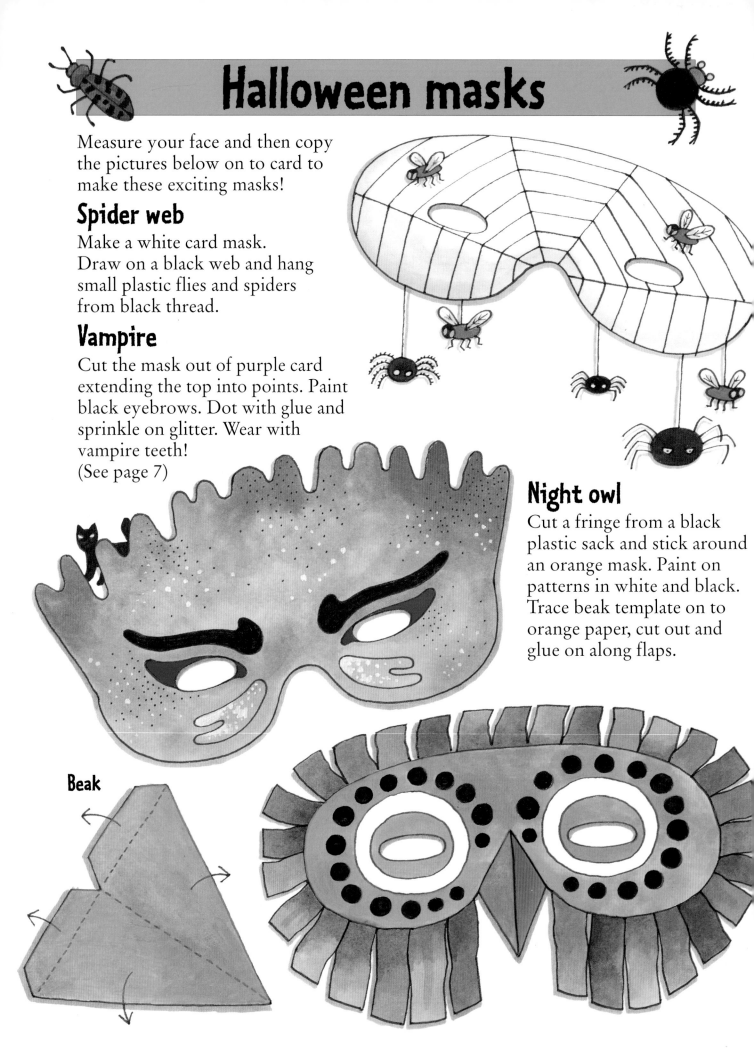

Toffee apples

What you will need

★ 10 apples, washed and dried
★ 10 wooden sticks

For the toffee

★ 350 g soft brown sugar
★ 50 g butter
★ 100 g golden syrup
★ 1 tsp lemon juice
★ 150 ml water

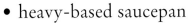

• heavy-based saucepan
• wooden spoon
• bowl of cold water
• oiled greaseproof paper

Ask a grown-up to help you make these as the toffee gets very hot.

1

Remove stalks and push sticks firmly into apples.

Put the toffee ingredients into the saucepan and heat gently until dissolved. Stir occasionally.

2

Increase the heat and boil rapidly until a dollop of toffee becomes hard when dropped into cold water.

3

Make sure they are completely covered in toffee.

Remove from heat. Carefully dip each apple in the toffee. Then plunge it into a bowl of cold water.

4

Stand the apples on oiled greaseproof paper until the toffee has set hard.

Spot the difference

Can you spot ten differences between these two pictures?

Eyeball cakes

What you will need

★ 100 g softened butter
★ 100 g caster sugar
★ 100 g self-raising flour
★ 2 eggs
★ 100 g icing sugar
★ small packet of chocolate buttons
★ red food colouring

• bowl
• wooden and metal spoons
• 18 paper cake cases
• bun tin
• small brush

1

Cream the butter and sugar together until pale in colour and fluffy.

2

Beat in the eggs one at a time with a tablespoon of flour with each. Fold in rest of flour with metal spoon.

3

Cool on wire rack.

Spoon equal amounts into 18 paper cases standing in bun tin. Bake in the oven at 190°C/375°F or Gas 5 for 20 minutes until risen and golden.

4

Mix 100 g of icing sugar with 1 tablespoon of hot water until smooth.

When cool, cover top of cakes with icing. Place a chocolate button in centre. With the small brush draw veins on icing in red food colouring.

Creepy mobile

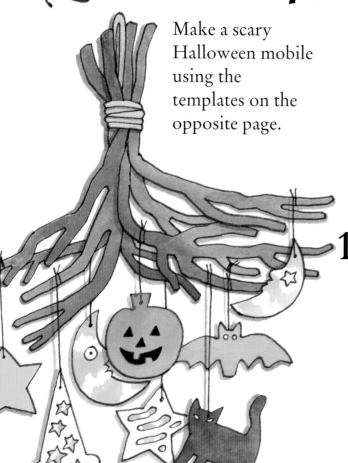

Make a scary Halloween mobile using the templates on the opposite page.

What you will need

★ thin card or stiff paper
★ pencil and tracing paper
★ scissors
★ paint and brushes
★ coloured foil or sticky shapes
★ needle and black thread
★ twigs tied in a bunch

1

See page 2 for how to trace templates.

Trace the templates on to the card or stiff paper and cut out. Make several of each shape.

2

Decorate with foil, paint and shapes – don't forget to do both sides.

3

Cut pieces of thread to different lengths.

Make a small hole at the top of each shape with the needle and thread. Pull thread through, knot and hang from twigs.

21

Pumpkin jellies

These jellies are great for Halloween parties. You could use any colour of jelly you like. Remember to ask a grown-up to help you with cutting the oranges.

What you will need
★ 5 oranges
★ 1 packet of green jelly

• sharp knife
• metal spoon
• bowl
• measuring jug
• wooden spoon

1

Ask a grown-up to help you cut the top off each orange with a sharp knife. Scoop out the flesh carefully and eat!

2

Cut faces with the knife. Make jelly with a bit less water than it says on the packet and put in the fridge.

3

Cut a small piece off bottom to stand.

When the jelly is set mash it and fill each orange shell with some. Replace the lid.

22

Apple games

Apples have always been connected with Halloween and apple games are part of the fun. Here are a couple of games to play.

Apple bobbing

Fill a washing-up bowl with cold water. Place on a table and add lots of apples. Bend over the bowl with your hands behind your back and take turns at trying to pick up an apple in your mouth. Have a towel ready for drying!

Snap apples

Using a metal skewer make a hole through the centre of several apples. Push in some lengths of string and knot at the end. Tie the apples on to a length of rope or pole so they are at mouth height. The winner of this game is the one who finishes eating the apple first. Holding the apples is not allowed!

Halloween howlers

★ *What has feathers, fangs and goes 'quack'?*
Count Duckula.

★ *Why don't skeletons go to scary films?*
They don't have the guts.

★ *How does a witch tell the time?*
With a witchwatch.

★ *Why was Dracula put in jail?*
He tried to rob a blood bank.

★ *What's a ghost's favourite game?*
Hide and shriek!

★ *What's the best way to talk to a monster?*
Long distance.

★ *What goes ha, ha, ha, bonk?*
A monster laughing his head off.

★ *What's a vampire's favourite fruit?*
A blood orange.

Aaaaaaaaaahhhh!

WINTER

Before you begin

- Most projects in this book use things you will already have around your home. Just check the 'What you will need' list on each page before you start to make sure you have everything ready.
- Always take great care with sharp tools such as scissors, needles and knives.
- Always cover work surfaces with newspaper before you start to paint or use glue.
- Wash your hands and wear an apron before preparing food.

Some basic tools and materials:
paint and brushes
glue
scissors
wool and darning needle
card and paper
tracing paper and pencil

 A snowflake has drifted down on to each page. See if you can spot it as you go through the book.

Snowflakes

We get snow instead of rain in cold weather because at low temperatures water vapour in the air freezes into clusters of crystals – snowflakes.

Each one 'grows' from the centre outwards and each has six points, but they all have a unique pattern – like fingerprints – no two are the same.

When you are happy with your snowflake design, draw over it in pen. Then you can rub out the template guide lines.

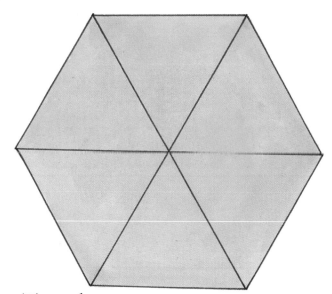

Template

Use this template as a starting point for your own snowflake design. Trace this shape on to tracing paper, then turn the paper over and scribble over the lines with a soft pencil. Turn the paper over again, tape it on to a piece of card or paper, and draw firmly over the lines again.

Tidy tray

Transform a shoe box into an attractive place to put away all the bits and pieces you've collected over the summer. You'll know where to find them for next year!

What you will need:

❊ shoe box
❊ corrugated card
❊ glue
❊ scissors
❊ piece of wrapping paper or wallpaper
❊ paints and brush
❊ felt tip pen

1

Measure a strip of paper long enough to wrap around the box, and add 2 cm. Make the strip 5 cm higher than the sides of the box. Cut it out.

2

Starting from a corner, stick the paper around the box leaving an overlap top and bottom. Fold over the edges of the paper and glue down.

3

Cut a piece of card to fit in the box, and about 10-15 cm taller. Draw a design on it and cut around the top of the shape.

4

Paint your design in bright colours. When it is dry, glue the card inside the box.

Recycle your old Christmas and birthday cards, postcards and photographs. Use them to create decorations of all shapes and sizes. The templates on the page opposite will help.

What you will need:
❋ wool
❋ large darning needle
❋ cards of all types
❋ scissors
❋ glue
❋ hole punch

Cut out pictures or photos and glue them on to coloured card of different shapes (see opposite page).

To make a new greetings card, cut two pieces the same shape and sew around their edges. Stitch them together along one edge, as shown below.

Use the darning needle and wool to sew around the edges of the card. Make stitches 5 mm from the edge and 5 mm apart. Use long pieces of wool so you don't have to tie on new pieces very often.

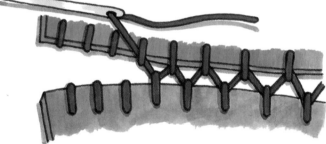

Mini-tassels

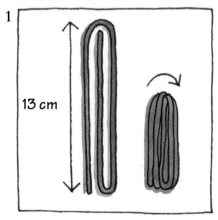

1

13 cm

Fold wool in three. Fold the bundle in half.

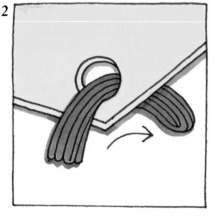

2

Push the folded end of the wool through a hole.

3

Pass the ends through the folded loop and pull firmly. Cut the ends off straight.

snowflake

triangle

star

Templates

Trace a shape on to tracing paper. Turn over and scribble over the shape with a soft pencil. Turn over again, place on card and draw firmly over the shape outline again. Remove the tracing paper and cut out the shape.

Don't trim the top loop, use it to hang your decoration.

Here are some ideas for using the templates, mini-tassels and stitching

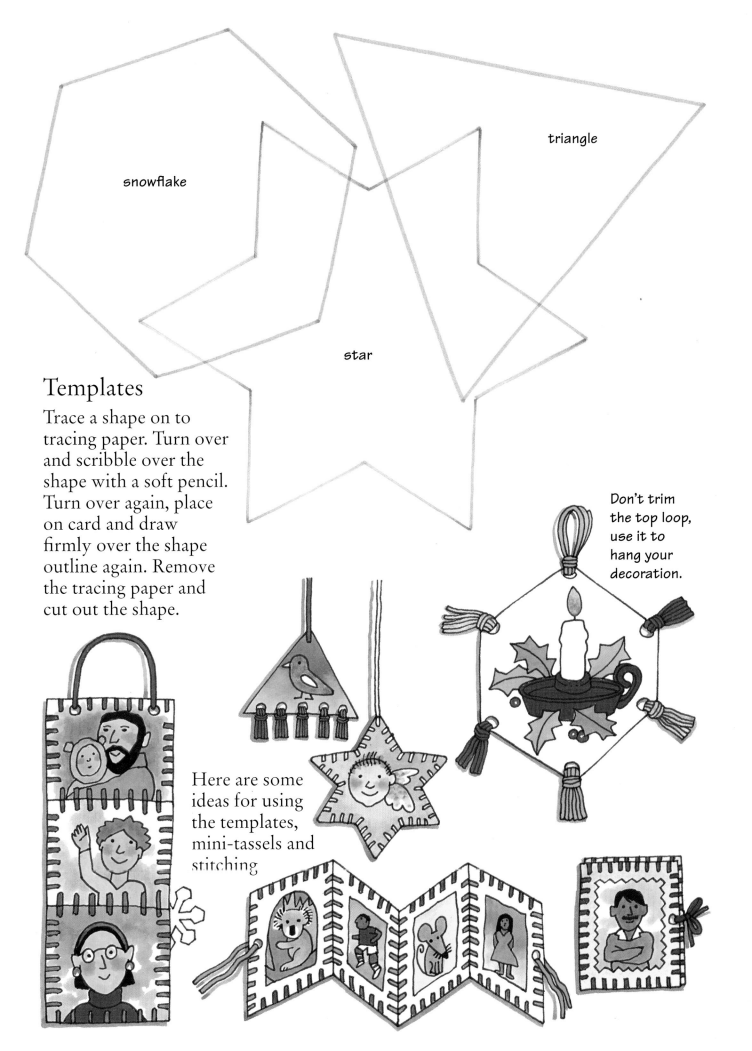

Blow football

Find a flat surface to play on and tape a cup on its side at each end of the 'playing field', about 50 cm apart. If you don't have a ball you can make one by scrunching up a piece of paper and wrapping it in sticky tape.

What you will need:
* ❄ 2 straws
* ❄ 2 paper or plastic cups
* ❄ sticky tape
* ❄ small light ball
  (e.g. ping pong ball)

Paint your cup in your favourite club colours

How to play

Place the ball in the centre of the pitch. At the signal each player tries to get a goal by blowing the ball towards their cup using a straw. The player who scores the most goals wins the match.

You can introduce as many real football rules as you like, for example changing ends at half time, taking penalty 'kicks', and so on.
If you run out of puff you can flick the ball with your finger.

Paper mosaics

Create a picture with small pieces of paper glued down on a card background.

What you will need:
❋ old magazines
❋ glue
❋ piece of card
❋ scissors
❋ pencil

Cut or tear different coloured papers into small pieces. Keep them in small piles of the same colour.

Draw a simple picture. Colour your drawing by sticking the small pieces of paper on it.

You could use coloured sticky shapes for the eyes.

For wintery scenes use cool colours such as blues and greys.
For warmer scenes use warm colours such as yellows, oranges and reds.

Combine cut and torn pieces of paper.

You could make a border around your picture with silver or coloured papers.

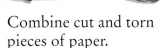

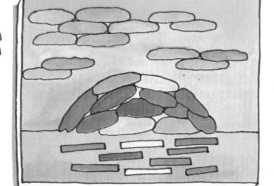

Use different shades of the same colours to create a beautiful sunset over the sea, for example.

Piggy bank

Make yourself a papier maché piggy bank and use the winter to start saving!

What you will need:
* balloon
* wallpaper paste
* old newspapers
* egg box
* sticky tape
* 2 plastic bowls
* wooden spoon
* thin card
* vaseline
* paint and brush
* craft knife

1

Blow up a balloon (not too full) and smear it all over with vaseline.

2

Tear up the newspaper into smallish strips and put into one of the bowls.

3

Mix up the wallpaper paste in the other bowl, following the instructions on the packet.

4

Stick the paper strips on to the balloon leaving the knot sticking out. Cover with several layers. Smooth down as you go along. Leave to dry.

5

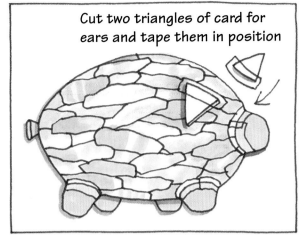

Cut two triangles of card for ears and tape them in position

Cut four legs and a snout from the egg box. Tape them in position.

6

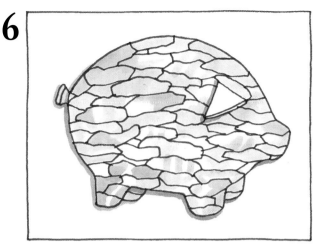

Cover the legs, snout and ears with paper until they are firmly attached.

7

Take care when using a craft knife

When the pig is completely dry, pop the balloon near the knot and pull it out. Paper over the hole. Carefully cut a slot in the top with a craft knife.

8

Paint your pig in bright colours. Add eyes, a tail, and a smile!

SAVING TIPS

Think of something to save for, like:
- a holiday
- a special treat
- Christmas

Try and put a regular amount into piggy each week

Earn a little money doing jobs at home

Every penny counts!

Pom-poms

Decorate your clothes and hair with these jolly woollen balls. Alter the size by using different-sized rings or by varying the thickness of the wool.

What you will need:
❋ wool
❋ thin card
❋ pair of compasses
❋ scissors
❋ darning needle

1
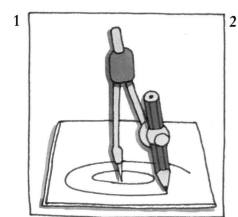

Draw a circle 3 cm across on a piece of card. Using the same centre point, draw another circle measuring 8 cm.

2

Cut out the ring and make a second one by drawing around the first. Place the two together.

3
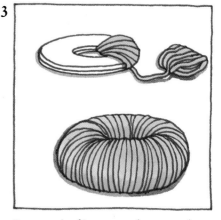

Start winding wool around the rings. Continue until the central hole is filled in.

4
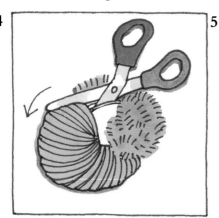

Push the point of the scissors between the wool and the two card rings. Cut the wool around the ring.

5
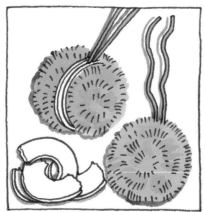

Push a 30 cm length of wool between the rings and tie tightly in a knot. Tear off the card rings and fluff out your pom-pom.

Tie on to hair bands of all kinds.

Use a darning needle to sew on to hats and scarves.

Wool tassels

These tassels will brighten up all kinds of things, from bags to cushions. Make multi-coloured ones, or make larger ones by lengthening the piece of card, or mini ones by shortening the card.

What you will need:
✳ wool
✳ card
✳ ruler and pencil
✳ scissors
✳ darning needle

1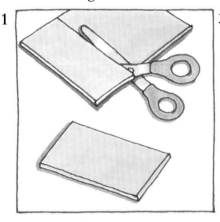

For a tassel 10 cm long, cut a piece of card 12 cm x 7 cm.

2

Wind wool around the card at least 20 times. The more times, the fatter the tassel.

3

Cut the wool along one edge of the card. Open the wool carefully and lie it out flat.

4

Lay a 40 cm length of wool on top. Tie around the middle tightly with another piece of wool.

5

Fold the bundle in two, with the long piece of wool coming out of the top.

6

Wind a 20 cm length of wool around the top of the tassel and knot tightly. Trim the bottom if necessary.

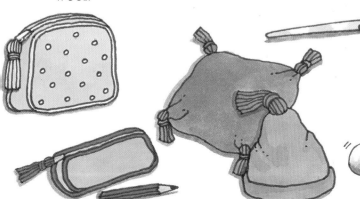

Use a darning needle to sew your tassels on to jumpers, cushions, hats and scarves.

Long ago winters were very hard in the Northern Hemisphere and many ancient festivals were to encourage the sun to regain its strength. As the weather was bad and the days were short, people had a long break from their farming and time to celebrate and look forward to warmer weather. Other traditional winter festivals celebrate the end of one year and the start of the next.

Christmas

This is the Christian celebration of the birth of Jesus Christ on December 25th. In churches and homes people put a 'crib', a model of the scene of the birth of baby Jesus in a stable. It shows Jesus's parents, Mary and Joseph, the three kings and shepherds who came to see the baby, and all the animals.

People also decorate the streets with lights and put a decorated fir tree in their homes. Families have a special meal together, either on Christmas Day or on Christmas Eve.

Chanukah

This is an eight-day festival in December when Jews celebrate the miracle of the lamp full of holy oil that burned for eight days, over 2000 years ago. They light one candle each day on a special eight-branched candlestick called a 'menorah'. Families have parties and eat potato pancakes called 'latkes'. Children receive small gifts on each of the eight days of the festival.

Id-ul-Fitr

This is the three-day Muslim festival to celebrate the end of Ramadan, the holy month. During Ramadan, Muslims have to fast (not eat) from sunrise until sunset. At Id people can eat when they want and there are special cakes, biscuits and sweets. They give money to the poor and send cards. The festival starts in December or January when the new moon is first spotted in the sky.

Chinese New Year

Chinese people all over the world celebrate the new year in late January or early February. They clean their houses thoroughly as it's a time to sweep away bad things from the old year. The special new year colours are red for good luck and gold for plenty. Huge dragons lead street processions and people let off fireworks.

New Year's Day

This is the 1st January, the start of the new year. The night before, on New Year's Eve, people celebrate with parties. At the stroke of midnight they drink a toast, kiss each other, and often make a lot of noise with singing and fireworks. If you make a 'new year's resolution' you try and break a bad habit or start a good one in the year to come.

St. Valentine's Day

On 14th February, people celebrate love. They send cards decorated with hearts to those they love, unsigned, so their love is kept secret.

On February 15th, in an ancient Roman festival, young men chose a girl by pulling names out of a big jar. Is this the origin of St Valentine's Day?

Pretzels

These are best eaten straight away, warm from the oven, but they will keep for up to a week in an airtight tin. Makes about 12.

You could also try making letters or numbers

What you will need

❅ 1 envelope dried yeast
❅ 4 tablespoons warm water
❅ 1 tablespoon golden syrup
❅ 1 teaspoon each of salt and sea salt
❅ 175 g whole wheat flour
❅ 1 beaten egg, and a brush
❅ mixing bowl and wooden spoon
❅ baking tray

1

Preheat the oven to 425°F/220°C or gas mark 7. In the mixing bowl, dissolve the yeast in the warm water.

2

Add the syrup and salt (not sea salt). Mix well. Stir in the flour. Knead the dough on a floured surface.

3

Roll the dough into snakes. Form into pretzel shapes (twists) and place on baking tray.

4

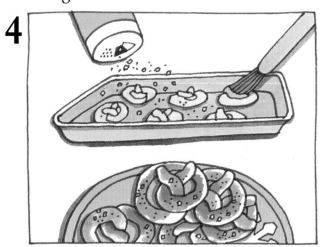

Brush with egg and sprinkle with sea salt. Cook in the centre of the oven for about 10 minutes. Take care – the oven will be hot!

Chocolate fudge

Really delicious, and very quick and easy to make. Give some as a present.

What you will need
* ❋ 100g plain chocolate
* ❋ 50g butter
* ❋ 3 tablespoons single cream
* ❋ 1 teaspoon vanilla essence
* ❋ 450g icing sugar
* ❋ small saucepan and bowl
* ❋ wooden spoon and sieve
* ❋ 20 cm square baking tin

1

Take care!
Ask an adult to help.

Break up the chocolate and put into the bowl with the butter. Place over a saucepan of simmering water, stirring occasionally.

2

When melted, turn off the heat and remove the bowl from the saucepan. Stir in the cream and vanilla essence.

3

Slowly add the sieved icing sugar, mixing well until thick and chocolatey.

4

Butter the baking tin and press the fudge into it. Cool it in the fridge until it is set firm. Cut it into pieces.

Fleece hat and scarf

Fleece is wonderfully easy to work with. It is stretchy, doesn't fray when cut, and doesn't have a 'wrong' side. You can leave your hat and scarf plain or decorate them using the ideas on the page opposite.

What you will need:

❋ ⅓ metre fleece, 150cm wide (60")
❋ sewing machine or needle and thread
❋ tracing paper
❋ pencil
❋ scissors
❋ pins

Guide for cutting out

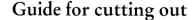
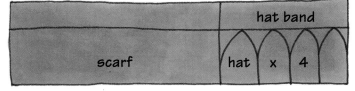

1

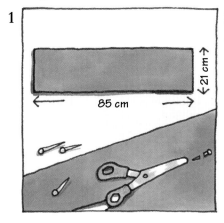

Lay out the fabric on a flat surface. Measure out the scarf and mark with pins. Cut out.

2

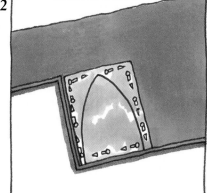

Trace the hat template on to tracing paper. Pin to the bottom edge of the fabric.

3

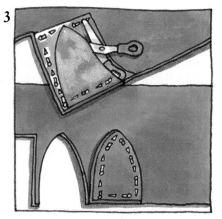

Cut through the paper and fleece. Cut another three using the first one.

4

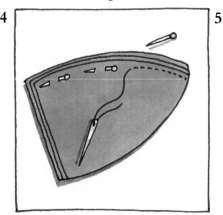

Pin the curved edges of two pieces together and sew together 5 mm from the edge.

5

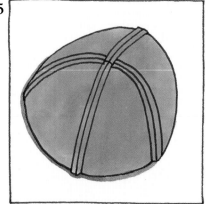

Attach the remaining three pieces in the same way, to form a domed shape.

6

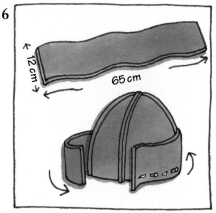

Cut a strip 12 cm x 65 cm from the remaining fleece. Pin it around the bottom of the hat. Start at a hat seam and leave 10mm of the strip sticking out at the beginning.

16

7

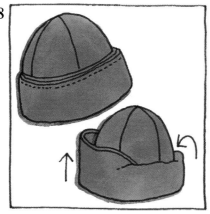

Sew the strip to the hat 5 mm in from the bottom edge. Sew the ends of the strip together and trim the ends if necessary.

8

Turn right-side out. Fold the strip up over the hat and tuck in the top edge to form a thick band.

Decoration

Decorate the band of the hat (sewing through the two layers), and the ends of the scarf. Remember that your stitching will show on both sides of the scarf. To make pompoms and tassels, see pages 10 and 11.

Wool stitching

Use coloured wool and a darning needle to decorate your hat and scarf with simple stitching.

Buttons

You could sew a row of buttons for decoration. Sew buttons on each side of the scarf in the same position.

Hat template

Use small jars such as baby food jars, with good screw-top lids. Clean and dry them and remove all labels. When you choose the toy make sure it fits nicely in the jar. It must have a flat base for gluing, and remember the bottom will be hidden by the lid.

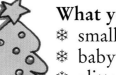

What you will need:
* ❋ small glass jar
* ❋ baby oil
* ❋ glitter or small sequins
* ❋ small toy or decoration
* ❋ glue

1

Carefully fill the jar with the oil.

2

Add some glitter or small sequins (or both!) to the oil.

3

Glue the small toy to the centre inside of the lid. Add glue around the inside edge of the lid then screw it tightly on to the jar.

4

Leave time for the glue to dry. Then turn the jar upside down and give it a shake. Watch the 'snow' swirling.

For most creatures winter is a hard time to find food and keep warm and dry. Some hibernate (go into a deep sleep) and some migrate to warmer countries for the winter months. However there are some animals who have adapted to survive winter in the Arctic, the coldest time in the coldest part of the world. Some fish and plants have also adapted so they can live in these harsh conditions.

Reindeer

These remarkably hardy animals live in the Arctic. Their thick waterproof coats keep them warm even in blizzards. They have hooves with a sharp cutting edge to dig through snow and ice for lichen to eat.

Polar bear

The bears have a dense furry winter coat and a layer of fat up to 10 cm thick to keep them warm. Their creamy white fur is good camouflage in the snow, and it repels water to keep them dry. They have no eyelashes because they would freeze, and a third eyelid protects them from snow blindness caused by bright reflections bouncing off the snow.

Female polar bears have their cubs in a snow den in December or January and don't bring them out until March, when it's warmer.

Musk ox

Musk ox have a fantastic woolly coat to protect them from the most severe cold. It has an undercoat of dense wool and an outer coat of long hair reaching almost to the ground.

Warming drinks

Hot spiced milk

for **4** people

What you will need:
* 750 ml milk
* 2 level tablespoons black treacle
* small pot double cream
* ground cinnamon
* saucepan, spoon, and 4 mugs

1 Take care! Ask an adult to help.

Put the milk and treacle into the saucepan and warm gently.

2

Pour into four mugs. Stir briskly, then pour the cream over the back of the spoon into each mug.

3

Sprinkle lightly with cinnamon.

Chocolate marshmallow floats

What you will need:
* 750 ml milk
* 2 heaped tablespoons drinking chocolate
* 8 marshmallows
* saucepan and 4 mugs
* whisk or fork

1 Take care! Ask an adult to help.

Pour the milk into the saucepan and heat gently. Remove from the heat.

2

Add the drinking chocolate to the milk. Whisk.

3

Pour into four mugs. Float two marshmallows on top of each drink.

Spot the difference

Can you spot ten differences between these two pictures?

Here are a few games to play indoors
when it's too cold and wet to play outside.

Wari

For 2 players

What you will need:
❄ 2 egg boxes
❄ 2 jar lids
❄ piece of card
❄ glue and scissors
❄ 48 dried beans or other small items
❄ paint or pens

1

Cut the lids off the egg boxes.
Glue the bases side by side in
the centre of the card.

2
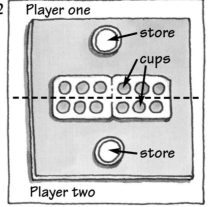

Glue the two jar lids
upside-down on to the card,
one on either side of the
boxes. These are the 'stores'.

3

Cut the card into a nice
shape. Paint and decorate
the board in bright colours.

How to play

❄ Each player has 24 beans. A player
sits either side of the board and
puts 4 beans into *each* of the cups
on his side.

❄ The first player takes the 4 beans
out of any cup on his side and,
going anti-clockwise, places 1 bean
in the next cup along, until they
are finished. You can go round
to the other player's side.

❄ The second player then takes 4
beans out of one of his cups and
moves along anti-clockwise, in
the same way.

❄ Whenever a player's *last* bean falls
into an opponent's cup so that the
total number of beans in the cup is
2 or 3 he takes these, plus any 2s or
3s in the cup *immediately* before it,
and puts them all in his store.

❄ The game carries on until no more
beans can be taken. Any beans left
belong to the player whose side
they are on.

❄ The player with the most beans
in his store wins.

Dice games

*For 2 or more players, or
on your own against the clock!*

Strike midnight

What you will need:

❋ 2 dice
❋ paper and pencils

How to play

❋ Each player draws a circle for a
  clockface on their piece of paper.
❋ The object of the game is to fill in
  the numbers on your clockface in
  order, starting with 1 and ending
  with 12.
❋ Take turns to throw one die.
  When you get 1, write it on to
  your clockface in the correct
  position. Continue taking it in
  turns to throw.
❋ When you reach 6, start throwing
  both dice and adding the two
  numbers together.
❋ The winner is the first person
  to reach midnight.

Lucky numbers

What you will need:

❋ 2 dice

How to play

❋ Each player chooses a lucky
  number between 2 and 12.
❋ Take turns to throw the dice and
  add up the total showing.
❋ The winner is the player who
  throws their lucky number the
  most times in 10 or 20 turns.

The faster you play the quicker you
have to add up!

23

Winter rhymes and jokes

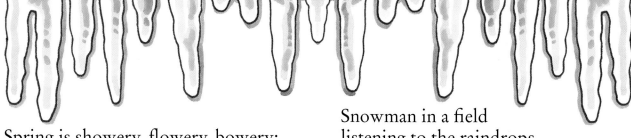

Spring is showery, flowery, bowery;
Summer is hoppy, croppy, poppy;
Autumn is slippy, drippy, nippy;
Winter is wheezy, sneezy, freezy.

                          Anon.

The north wind doth blow,
And we shall have snow,
And what will the robin do then,
       poor thing?
He'll sit in the barn,
And keep himself warm,
And hide his head under his wing,
       poor thing!

                          Anon.

Snowman in a field
listening to the raindrops
Wishing him farewell.

                   a Japanese haiku.

What do you call a sunburned snowman?
Water.

What story do snowmen like to tell their children?
Coldilocks and the three brrrs.

Knock, knock.
Who's there?
Lettuce.
Lettuce who?
Lettuce in, it's cold out here!

What do snowmen eat for breakfast?
SNOWflakes.

24

CHRISTMAS

Christmas fun

On the following pages you'll find lots of ideas for things to make to brighten up your Christmas.

And you can take a break from all that busy activity to enjoy these games and puzzles:

On page 24, you will find out how people celebrate Christmas around the world.

This Christmas robin will be hopping through the book with you.
See if you can spot him on each page.

What you need

★ Always take great care with sharp tools such as scissors, staplers, needles, and so on.

★ This symbol is to remind you to take extra care when you use these sharp tools.

★ When you use a craft knife, always put cardboard, hardboard or lino under your work. Hold your work firmly with one hand and cut away from you.

Some basic tools and materials:
paint
glue
scissors
different colour paper
different colour card
wax crayons
coloured pencils
felt-tip pens
stapler

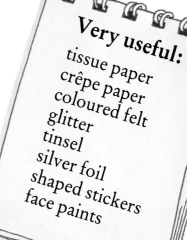

Very useful:
tissue paper
crêpe paper
coloured felt
glitter
tinsel
silver foil
shaped stickers
face paints

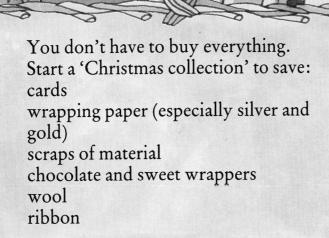

You don't have to buy everything.
Start a 'Christmas collection' to save:
cards
wrapping paper (especially silver and gold)
scraps of material
chocolate and sweet wrappers
wool
ribbon

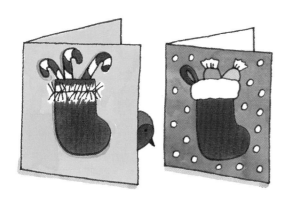

Stocking collage

What you will need

★ card
★ scissors
★ glue
★ scrap of red felt
★ silver foil or silver sweet wrapper
★ thin ribbon or paper ribbon
★ glitter
★ felt-tip pen (for message)
★ sweets or small gifts

BEFORE YOU BEGIN

Cut a piece of card.

Fold the card in half.

If you use paper,
fold it into four.

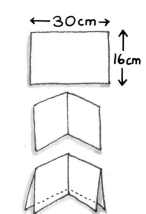

1

Take a piece of red felt. Cut out the shape of a thick stocking.

2

Leave space above stocking

Don't glue here

Glue   Glue

Glue the edge of the stocking. Stick it on the card. Leave the top open.

3

Dab glue and

Fill with sweets

Write message inside

around card

sprinkle glitter

Cut a strip of silver foil and tie a ribbon. Glue them along the top of the stocking.

Star stencil

Once you have made your stencil, you can print several of these cards.

What you will need

★ newspaper (for protection)
★ dark colour card (for card)
★ any colour thick card (for stencil)
★ craft knife or sharp scissors – take great care!
★ white or yellow poster paint
★ sponge or paintbrush
★ glue
★ glitter
★ felt-tip pen (for message)

BEFORE YOU BEGIN
Cover a table or the floor with newspaper. Put on an apron or overalls.
Check how to use a craft knife on page 5.

1

if you can.
Use star template
to be perfect.
star shape doesn't have

Make a stencil. Draw a star on thick card and cut around it.

2

You could splatter paint with a brush

Put the stencil over the front of your card. Sponge on the paint.

3

Write message inside

Dab glue around the edge of the star. Sprinkle glitter on to the glue.

Gift tags

Here are three ways of making pretty gift tags.

What you will need

★ old Christmas cards
★ scissors
★ hole puncher
★ pieces of card
★ shaped stickers
★ glitter
★ felt-tip pen (for message)
★ for potato prints - see page 14

1

Cut up old Christmas cards. Choose parts with no writing on the back.

to Grandma
Happy Christmas
love Ka
xxx

Use a hole puncher to punch a hole. Thread wool through the hole.

2

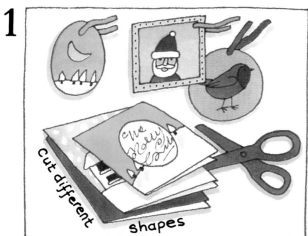

Cut small rectangles from card. Make a pattern with shaped stickers.

3

Add glitter

Cut small rectangles of card. Print shapes with potato cuttings. Look at pages 14 and 15 for how to do it.

Away in a manger

Can you spot ten differences between these two pictures?

Two paper chains

What you will need

★ different wrapping paper
★ 2 rolls of different colour crêpe paper
★ scissors
★ glue or double-sided tape

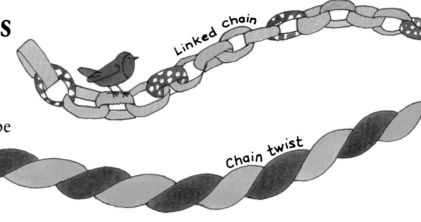

Linked chain

Chain twist

1

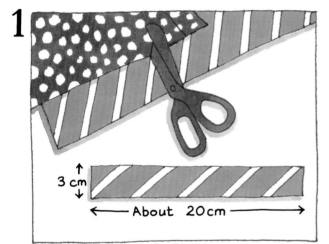

3 cm

← About 20 cm →

Cut strips of different wrapping paper.

2

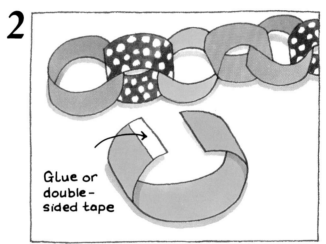

Glue or double-sided tape

Glue each strip together to link the chain.

1

3cm wide

Cut a strip from the end of two rolls of different colour crêpe paper.

2

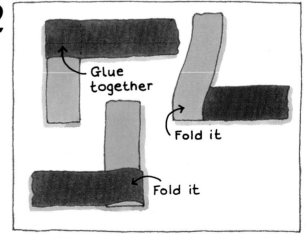

Glue together

Fold it

Fold it

Glue the ends together. Fold one strip over the other. Glue the end. Stretch it.

1

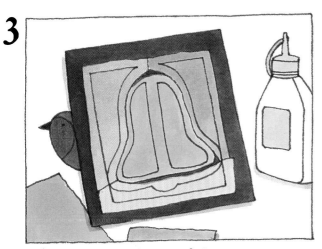

Cut a rectangle of black paper. Draw a frame and bell shape in chalk.

2

Cut out the bell shape. Make sure it touches the frame on 3 sides.

3

Glue or tape pieces of tissue paper to the back. Use different colours.

Stained glass window

What you will need

★ thick black paper
★ chalk or white crayon
★ craft knife or sharp scissors - take great care!
★ coloured tissue paper
★ glue or sticky tape
★ string

BEFORE YOU BEGIN
Check how to use a craft knife on page 5.

String

Hole

Hang it in your bedroom window

Lanterns

What you will need

★ old wrapping paper, coloured paper or coloured foil
★ pencil
★ ruler
★ scissors
★ glue

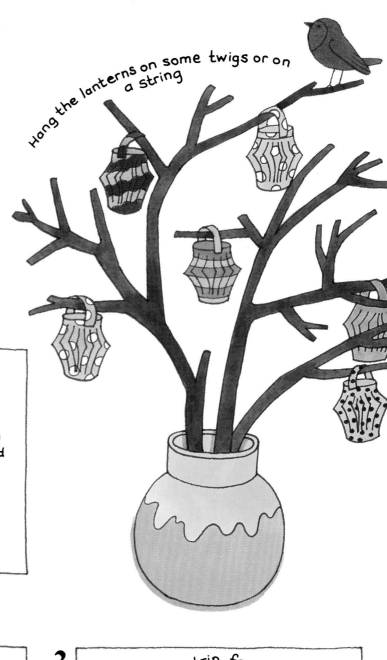

Hang the lanterns on some twigs or on a string

1

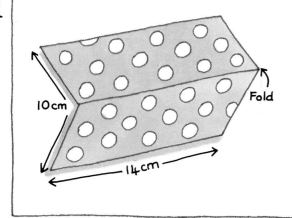

10 cm

14 cm

Fold

Cut a rectangle from wrapping paper, coloured paper or foil.

2

Leave 1 cm

Fold it in half. Cut narrow strips along the fold. Don't cut to the edge.

3

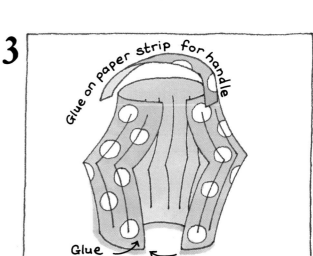

Glue on paper strip for handle

Glue

Open the paper out. Curve it round and glue the edges together.

10

Tricky trees

Each of these Christmas trees has one thing missing.
Can you see what it is?

Journey to Bethlehem

This is a game for 2-3 players.
You will need 3 counters and a die.
Mary and Joseph, the three kings, and the shepherds, are all travelling to Bethlehem. Which group will arrive first? Pick a group. The youngest can start, then the player on their right. Throw the die to move along the board. The winner is the first to the stable.
Do you know who reached the stable first in the real Nativity story?
Do you know why Mary and Joseph were travelling to Bethlehem?

Mary and Joseph

1 2 3 4 5 6

Donkey still fresh.
Go forward 4.

Road passes through valley.
Go forward 6.

7 8 9 10 11 12 13 14 15 16

Mary too stiff to ride.
Miss a turn.

Lose lamb.
Miss a turn.

8 9 10 11 12

Path goes downhill.
Go forward 6.

7

6

5

Excited by angel's words.
Go forward 4.

4

3

Take wrong road.
Go back 2.

2

1

13 14 15 16 17 18 19 20 21

Take short cut.
Go forward 3.

Joseph offered lift in cart.
Go forward 3.

Stop for rest.
Miss a turn.

22 23

Carry smallest lamb.
Go forward 2.

24 25 26

Shepherds

3 Kings

Star shines brightly.
Go forward 4.

Well-trodden track.
Go forward 6.

Stuck in sand dune.
Miss a turn.

Don't stop for rest.
Go forward 3.

Leave frankincense at picnic spot.
Go back 2.

Fresh water at oasis.
Go forward 2.

Camel lame.
Miss a turn.

Get lost in mountains.
Go back 2.

See Bethlehem in distance.
Go forward 2.

Mary too tired to travel.
Miss a turn.

Cloudy night, no star.
Go back 1.

NO ROOM

No room at inn.
Go back 1.

Can't find stable.
Go back 1.

Christmas wrapping paper

Potato print

What you will need

★ newspaper (for protection)
★ large sheets of paper
★ poster paints in bright colours
★ saucers (one for each colour)
★ one large potato
★ sharp kitchen knife
★ glitter (if you want)
★ silver pen (if you want)

BEFORE YOU BEGIN
Put on an apron or overalls. Cover your working surface with newspaper. Cover another surface (extra table or floor) with newspaper for drying your work.

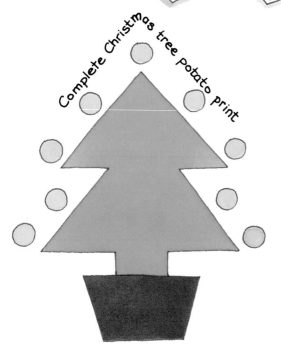

Complete Christmas tree potato print

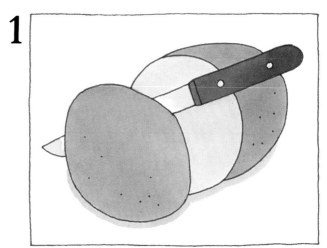

1

First ask a grown-up to help you cut the potato. Cut 2 thick slices.

2

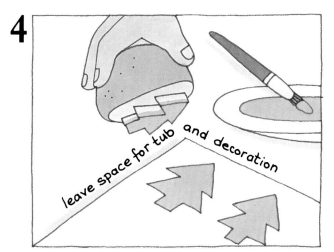

Cut the simple shapes. Use a trimming for the decoration.

3

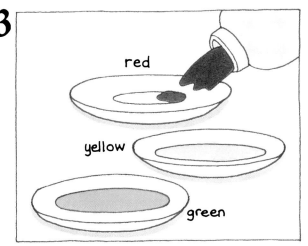

Pour a small amount of paint into each saucer.

4

Dip the shape into the paint and print all over the paper.

5

Add the tubs and then the decorations. Put the sheet to dry.

6

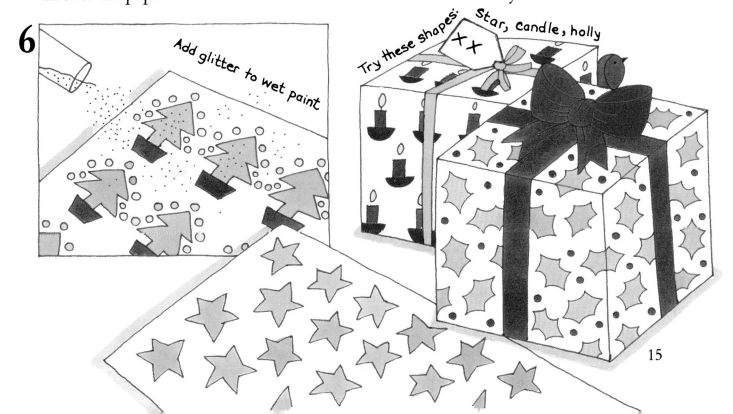

15

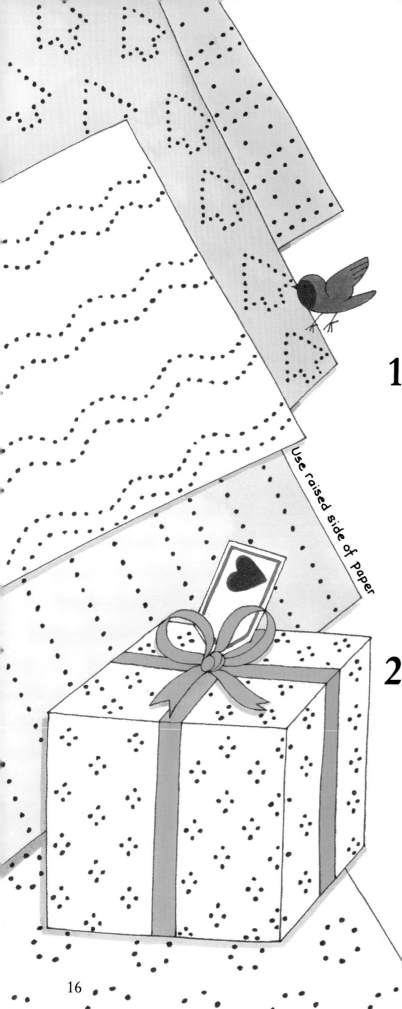

Use raised side of paper

Pattern of holes

What you will need

★ large sheet of coloured paper
★ thin knitting needle or very sharp pencil
★ thick rug or blanket

1

Put the paper on a thick rug or folded blanket. Hold the edges firmly.

2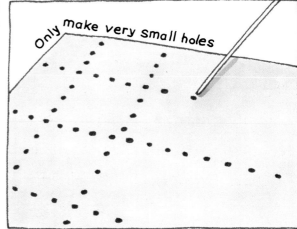

Only make very small holes

Push the knitting needle or sharp pencil through the paper. Try to make a pattern.

16

Gifts galore

Each of these presents has a pair – except one.
Can you spot the odd one out?

Desk tidier

This could be for your teacher or a friend at school, or for one of your family.

What you will need

★ toilet roll tubes (at least 4)
★ scissors
★ old wrapping paper or silver foil
★ glue
★ light card
★ pencil

Cut one very short

Cut 4 or 5 toilet roll tubes to different lengths.

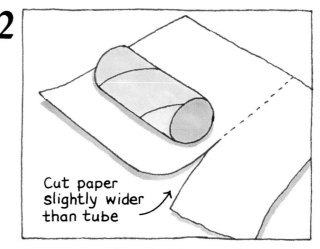

Cut paper slightly wider than tube ↗

Cut rectangles of old wrapping paper or silver foil to cover the tubes.

3

Snip the ends of the paper.

4

Glue
down

Glue the paper to the tubes and tuck the ends in firmly.

5

Put the tubes on a flat surface and glue them together.

6

Take a piece of card and draw round the bottom of the tubes.

7

Cut out the shape

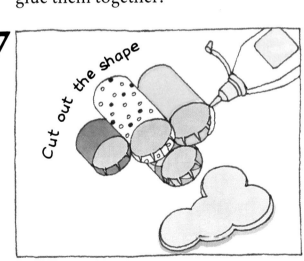

Glue the shaped card to the bottom of the tubes.

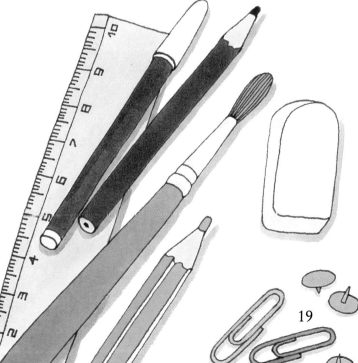

Christmas badges

What you will need

★ light card
★ Christmas templates (if you want)
★ pencil
★ scissors
★ crayons, paints, stickers, glitter, holly (for decoration)
★ felt-tip pen (for message)
★ sticky tape
★ double-sided tape
★ safety pin

1

Draw, then cut out the shape of the badge. Use templates if you want.

2

Decorate the front of the badge and write a message.

3

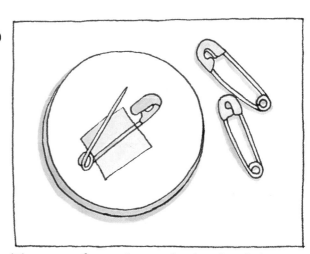

Tape a safety pin to the back of the badge. Close it carefully.

HAPPY CHRISTMAS

DAD

Make a giant badge with a paper plate

Stick a badge on a card

NOEL

20

Christmas cooking

Give these as presents for your teachers or friends

Chocolate snowballs

What you will need

These quantities make about 15 walnut-sized balls.
- ★ 100 g plain cooking chocolate
- ★ 150 g stoned dates, chopped
- ★ 100 g dried apricots, chopped finely (soak first to moisten)
- ★ 50 g chopped mixed nuts
- ★ desiccated coconut
- ★ sugar strands (hundreds and thousands)
- ★ drinking chocolate or cocoa powder
- ★ mixing bowl
- ★ fork
- ★ paper sweet cases

BEFORE YOU BEGIN
Wash your hands and put on an apron or overall. Take out all things you will need.

1

Use a dish over boiling water

Ask a grown-up to help you melt the chocolate.

2

Use a fork to mix

Mash together the melted chocolate, dates, apricots, and nuts.

3

Put in paper sweet cases, chill in fridge

Form the mixture into little balls. Roll them in the coconut, hundreds and thousands or chocolate powder.

Christmas present

What you will need

- ★ large cardboard box
- ★ scissors or craft knife – take extra care!
- ★ newspaper (for protection)
- ★ poster paints in bright colours
- ★ wide foil or paper ribbon
- ★ sticky tape or stapler
- ★ stickers, sequins, glitter, tinsel
- ★ hair-band
- ★ piece of white paper or card (for label)
- ★ felt-tip pen (for message)
- ★ wool

BEFORE YOU BEGIN
For painting, put on an apron or overall and cover a table or the floor with newspaper.
You may need help from a grown-up or friend.

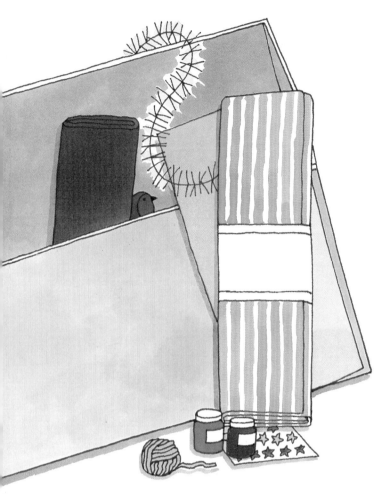

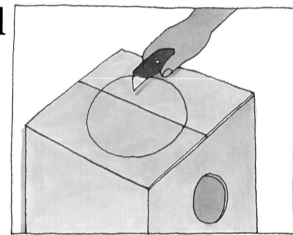

1 Cut a hole in the bottom of a large cardboard box. Cut 2 holes in the sides.

2 Paint the box a bright colour.

3

Tape or staple some wide ribbon across the box.

4

Decorate the box with stars, shaped stickers, silver or gold paint, or glitter.

5

Ask someone to help you

Lower the box carefully over your head. Put your arms through the sides.

6

Make a large ribbon bow. Tape it to a hair-band.

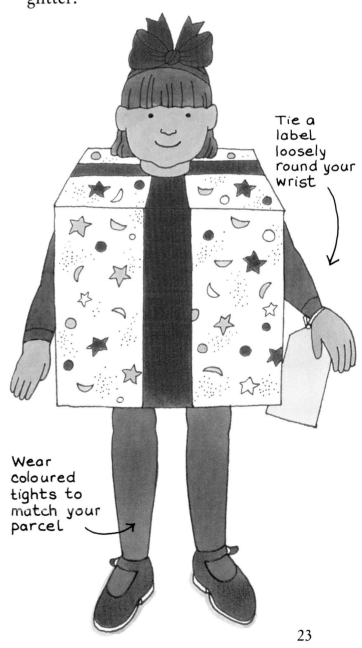

Tie a label loosely round your wrist

Wear coloured tights to match your parcel

Christmas around the world

Christmas is not only celebrated on December 25th. In the Netherlands and Belgium, children expect Santa Claus on the night before St Nicholas's day, December 6th. And on January 6th in Austria, children dress up as the three kings and walk through the snowy streets collecting money and small gifts.

I T A L Y

The **presepio**, the crib or nativity scene, is the most important decoration in Italian homes and churches. In churches, they are often very large with lights and moving people.

A U S T R A L I A

Christmas in Australia is in the middle of summer. Families spend the holiday on the beach and eat a hot roast lunch!

D E N M A R K

Children in Denmark have a very special Advent Calendar. It is made of cloth instead of paper and is embroidered with the numbers 1 to 24. Each morning in December, children wake up to discover a small present pinned to the right number. Could you make a calendar like this next year?

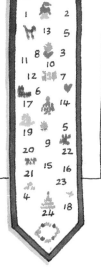

Happy Christmas!

Do you know how to say 'Happy Christmas' in Italian, French, German and Spanish? Which is which? The answers are upside down.

Buon Natale
Joyeux Noël
Feliz Navidad
Frohe Weihnachten

Frohe Weihnachten – German
Feliz Navidad – Spanish
Joyeux Noël – French
Buon Natale – Italian